NUCLEAR WASTE

The Biggest Clean-Up In History

Gary E. McCuen

IDEAS IN CONFLICT SERIES

GEM
GARY McCUEN

publications inc.

502 Second Street
Hudson, Wisconsin 54016
Phone (715) 386-7113

Illustration & photo credits

Web Bryant 87, Paul Conrad 69, Crowley 138, Englehart 55, Jerry Fearing 18, Jeff MacNelly 44, Sane/Freeze 126, David Seavey 82, Wayne Stayskal 110, United States Department of Energy 13, 39, 50, 64, 75, 93, 104, 119, United States General Accounting Office 24, 132. Cover illustration by Ron Swanson.

©1990 by Gary E. McCuen Publications, Inc.
502 Second Street, Hudson, Wisconsin 54016
(715) 386-7113
International Standard Book Number
0-86596-076-3
Printed in the United States of America

CONTENTS

CHAPTER 4 DECOMMISSIONING NUCLEAR POWER PLANTS

CHAPTER 5 THE NUCLEAR WEAPONS COMPLEX

REASONING SKILL DEVELOPMENT

These activities may be used as individualized study guides for students in libraries and resource centers or as discussion catalysts in small group and classroom discussions.

IDEAS in CONFLICT ®

This series features ideas in conflict on political, social and moral issues. It presents counterpoints, debates, opinions, commentary and analysis for use in libraries and classrooms. Each title in the series uses one or more of the following basic elements:

Introductions that present an issue overview giving historic background and/or a description of the controversy.

Counterpoints and debates carefully chosen from publications, books, and position papers on the political right and left to help librarians and teachers respond to requests that treatment of public issues be fair and balanced.

Symposiums and forums that go beyond debates that can polarize and oversimplify. These present commentary from across the political spectrum that reflect how complex issues attract many shades of opinion.

A global emphasis with foreign perspectives and surveys on various moral questions and political issues that will help readers to place subject matter in a less culture-bound and ethno-centric frame of reference. In an ever shrinking and interdependent world, understanding and cooperation are essential. Many issues are global in nature and can be effectively dealt with only by common efforts and international understanding.

Reasoning skill study guides and discussion activities provide ready made tools for helping with critical reading and evaluation of content. The guides and activities deal with one or more of the following:

RECOGNIZING AUTHOR'S POINT OF VIEW

INTERPRETING EDITORIAL CARTOONS

VALUES IN CONFLICT

WHAT IS EDITORIAL BIAS?

WHAT IS SEX BIAS?
WHAT IS POLITICAL BIAS?
WHAT IS ETHNOCENTRIC BIAS?
WHAT IS RACE BIAS?
WHAT IS RELIGIOUS BIAS?

*From across **the political spectrum** varied sources are presented for research projects and classroom discussions. Diverse opinions in the series come from magazines, newspapers, syndicated columnists, books, political speeches, foreign nations, and position papers by corporations and non-profit institutions.*

About the Editor

Gary E. McCuen is an editor and publisher of anthologies for public libraries and curriculum materials for schools. Over the past 19 years his publications of over 200 titles have specialized in social, moral and political conflict. They include books, pamphlets, cassettes, tabloids, filmstrips and simulation games, many of them designed from his curriculums during 11 years of teaching junior and senior high school social studies. At present he is the editor and publisher of the *Ideas in Conflict* series and the *Editorial Forum* series.

CHAPTER 1

NUCLEAR WASTE OVERVIEW

1   NUCLEAR WASTE OVERVIEW

DISPOSING OF NUCLEAR WASTE

Carl E. Behrens

Carl E. Behrens is an environmental researcher and analyst in the Environmental and Natural Resources Policy Division of the Library of Congress. This statement was excerpted from his article on nuclear waste disposal.

Points to Consider:

1. Describe the several types of nuclear waste and the hazards they present.

2. What are the sources of nuclear waste?

3. How did the Nuclear Waste Policy Act attempt to provide direction to the nuclear waste program? What prompted Congress to redirect the waste program in 1987?

4. Describe the Waste Isolation Pilot Project. What purpose will it serve?

Carl E. Behrens, "Nuclear Waste Disposal," *CRS Issue Brief,* January 11, 1988, The Library of Congress.

The goal of the nuclear waste program is to develop a deep geological waste repository where spent fuel may be placed permanently and require no monitoring after it [the repository] is filled and closed. Choosing a site for a waste repository has become the most controversial aspect of the nuclear waste issue.

Disposal of radioactive waste has been one of the most enduring controversies about commercial nuclear power. After many years of delay in the national nuclear waste program, Congress passed the comprehensive Nuclear Waste Policy Act of 1982. The Act detailed procedures for the Department of Energy (DOE) in siting and constructing repositories for spent nuclear fuel and high-level waste. By 1986, however, DOE's waste program had raised so much discontent that Congress imposed a virtual moratorium on further progress in the Fiscal Year 1987 continuing resolution. At issue: should Congress order DOE to pursue the waste program defined by the 1982 law, or should Congress change it [the program]?

Radioactive Waste: What It Is and Where It Comes From

There are several types of nuclear waste, and they vary in the degree of hazard they present and the length of time they remain hazardous.

1. *Spent reactor fuel and high-level waste* are the most significant types of radioactive waste. They contain high concentrations of toxic radioactive fission products, which decay to safe levels within 600–700 years. They also contain plutonium and other "transuranic" (TRU) elements, some of which remain radioactively hazardous for many thousands of years.

2. *Low-level waste* contains fission products but no TRU elements. The concentration of radioactivity is much lower, and its hazardous life is measured in hundreds rather than thousands of years.

3. *Low-level TRU waste* is contaminated with low concentrations of TRU radioactivity. Its radioactive life is thus comparable to that of spent fuel or high-level waste, although its hazardous content is much lower.

4. *Uranium mill tailings* are wastes from the process of refining ore to extract uranium. The tailings contain significant amounts of natural radium, which occurs in deposits of uranium

ore. Radium decays slowly but steadily into radon, a radioactive gas. Radon in turn decays into particles of radioactive "daughters" that can be hazardous if they collect in the basements of buildings. Mill tailings are less concentrated even than low-level waste, but their large volume and long radioactive life present special disposal problems.

Sources of Nuclear Waste

Most radioactive waste results from the operation of nuclear reactors. Commercial power reactors and reactors that produce plutonium for the weapons program are the primary sources, with naval propulsion reactors and small research reactors contributing a lesser amount. Industrial, research, and medical uses of radioactive materials create significant amounts of low-level waste. . . .

Waste from Commercial Power Reactors

Nuclear power reactors produce spent fuel and low-level waste, and the mining and milling of the uranium they use result in radioactive mill tailings.

Natural uranium consists of two types of isotopes: U-235, which fissions or splits easily, and U-238, which does not. When U-235 fissions it releases energy, which is the source of electric generating power in a commercial nuclear reactor. Natural uranium consists of less than 1 percent U-235, with the rest U-238.

Commercial power reactors in the United States use uranium that is enriched to about 3 percent U-235 by an enrichment plant. The enriched uranium is then formed into pellets and inserted in fuel rods for the reactor. Up to this stage, except for the mill tailings, there is very little radioactivity associated with the nuclear fuel cycle.

In the reactor, some of the U-235 fissions, which releases heat energy to run the turbines and generate electricity. The fragments of the fissioned U-235 atoms — called fission products — are radioactive elements lighter then uranium, such as strontium 90, cesium 137, and krypton 85.

In addition to the fission of U-235, another reaction takes place in the reactor: some of the U-238 absorbs a neutron and transmutes into plutonium.

Plutonium, like U-235, fissions readily. (There are several isotopes of plutonium; Pu-239 is the isotope that fissions most readily.) Thus, both U-235 and plutonium can be nuclear fuels, and early expectations were that plutonium would eventually be the main power fuel. With the slow-down in nuclear construction of the past decade, however, plutonium fuel does not appear likely to be economical, and there are no plans at present to use plutonium as a fuel in commercial U.S. power reactors. . . .

Spent Fuel

After fuel has been in a power reactor about three years, the concentration of U-235 atoms is reduced, and the fuel must be replaced. It contains mostly uranium, in which the U-235 has been depleted to about 1 percent. It also contains 2 percent highly radioactive fission products, and about 2 percent plutonium, transmuted from U-238 atoms.

As it comes out of the reactor, spent fuel gives off large amounts of heat from the radioactive decay of its fission products, and must be stored under water in storage pools at the reactor site. After about five years of storage under water, however, the more active fission products have decayed enough so the spent fuel may be stored in properly designed containers and cooled by air circulation. These dry storage casks may be located either at the reactor site, or at a central location such as the proposed Monitored Retrievable Storage (MRS) facility. Because it remains dangerously radioactive, however, spent fuel must be continuously monitored wherever it is temporarily stored.

The goal of the nuclear waste program is to develop a deep geological waste repository where spent fuel may be placed permanently and require no monitoring after it [the repository] is

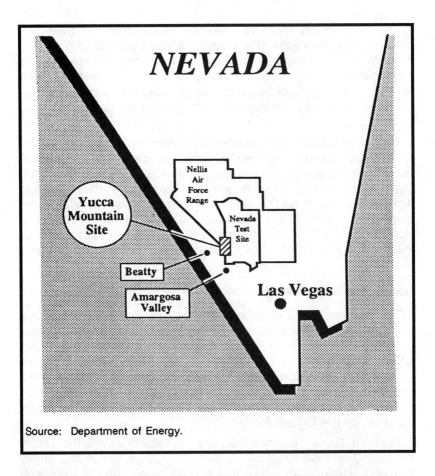

NEVADA

Nellis
Air
Force
Range

Nevada
Test
Site

Yucca
Mountain
Site

Beatty

Amargosa
Valley

Las Vegas

Source: Department of Energy.

filled and closed. Choosing a site for a waste repository has become the most controversial aspect of the nuclear waste issue.

Waste from Weapons Program Reactors

Reactors run by the Department of Energy to produce plutonium also produce waste similar to that from commercial power reactors. In fact, the N-Reactor at Hanford, Washington, is a dual-purpose facility, producing plutonium for weapons and also generating 850 megawatts of electricity for the commercial grid. The major difference is that the spent fuel from plutonium production reactors, instead of being stored for eventual disposal, is reprocessed to extract the plutonium and remaining uranium, leaving behind a solution of high-level radioactive fission products.

The production reactors use natural uranium, so their fuel cycle does not include enrichment. It does include mining and milling, with its accompanying mill tailings waste, and it produces low-level non-TRU waste like the commercial power plants. In addition, because of the reprocessing step, it creates low-level waste contaminated with plutonium and other TRU elements.

High-level waste from weapons production does not contain as much plutonium as does commercial spent fuel. However, reprocessing does not remove all the plutonium; about 0.5 percent remains. This is enough to require that defense high-level waste meet the same long-term disposal conditions as commercial spent fuel. TRU-contaminated low-level waste must also be disposed of in deep geologic repositories, rather than in the shallow land burial sites in which non-TRU low-level waste is placed.

Naval Propulsion and Research Reactors

The reactors used in submarines and other naval vessels are similar to power reactors, except that they use uranium fuel that is highly enriched in U-235 — in the range of 90 percent. This allows a high power output with a much smaller and lighter reactor, an important factor in naval propulsion. Many small research reactors, including some foreign research reactors built with U.S. cooperation, also operate on highly enriched uranium supplied by the United States.

Fuel for these reactors becomes inefficient when the U-235 concentration falls to about 75 percent. Since this is still highly enriched uranium, the spent fuel is reprocessed and the uranium is recycled through the enrichment plant to bring the concentration back up to 90 percent. As in the plutonium production cycle, reprocessing leaves behind high-level waste and low-level TRU waste that must be disposed of.

Industrial, Research, and Medical Uses of Radionuclides

Some of the fission products produced in nuclear reactors have uses in industry, medicine, and research. Use of such radionuclides and radiopharmaceuticals produces low-level waste similar to that produced by the operation of nuclear power plants, and this waste is disposed of in low-level burial grounds. . . .

Waste Management Programs

Responsibility for disposing of high-level radioactive waste, both from commercial nuclear power reactors and from weapons production reactors, has been consistently assigned to and accepted by the federal government, although the nuclear utilities are paying the cost of commercial waste disposal. Development of a waste disposal facility has been a long process with many changes in policy and direction, however, leaving a widespread impression that near-insuperable obstacles block safe disposal. This in turn has led to calls for (and, in some states, legislation) prohibiting construction of nuclear plants until demonstration of safe waste disposal.

On the other hand, most technical studies of waste disposal have expressed optimism, ranging from cautious to confident, that safe burial of radioactive wastes in the mined geological repository is technically feasible. . . .

The Nuclear Waste Policy Act

The 1982 Waste Policy Act attempted to provide direction to the nuclear waste program. It set up a procedure which DOE was to follow in identifying, "characterizing," and selecting two sites for permanent repositories, with the first to begin operation in 1998. The Act authorized construction of the first repository, but required separate authorization for the second. . . .

The Act also required DOE to report on the need for, and feasibility of, a Monitored Retrievable Storage (MRS) facility, and submit a proposal to construct one. The MRS would provide limited central storage of spent fuel before it was disposed of in a repository. . . .

Implementation of the Waste Policy Act

The Nuclear Waste Policy Act set many milestones for action by DOE and other agencies in developing the various waste facilities. In pursuing these milestones DOE identified nine sites in the West as potential candidates for the first repository, and identified three of them, in Texas, Nevada, and Washington, as preferred sites to be "characterized"—that is, to be explored in detail to determine geological structure through several thousand feet depth and suitability as a permanent repository. . . .

The Monitored Retrievable Storage (MRS) Facility

In the spring of 1985 DOE, following its directive in the Waste Policy Act, announced that an MRS facility could be useful not only for backup storage capacity but as a central receiving and waste preparation facility. It proposed three potential sites in Tennessee, including the site of the cancelled Clinch River

15

Breeder Reactor project.

Litigation initiated by the State of Tennessee prevented DOE from formally submitting the proposal to Congress until 1987. In March, the proposal finally came forward, but the general disarray of the DOE's waste program has precluded detailed attention to it.

Nuclear Waste Policy Amendments Act of 1987

In December 1987, as part of the budget reconciliation act of 1987, Congress redirected the waste program. Major features of the legislation, called the Nuclear Waste Policy Amendments Act of 1987, included:

- suspending all site-specific activity at all candidate sites except Yucca Mountain, Nevada;

- prohibiting any site-specific activities regarding a second repository, terminating research on crystalline rock, and reporting to Congress between 2007 and 2010 on the need for a second repository;

- authorizing construction of a Monitored Retrievable Storage (MRS) facility, but prohibiting selection of a site until a permanent repository site has been approved by the President;

- authorizing payment to Nevada of $10 million per year during siting and construction of the Yucca Mountain repository, and $20 million per year during operation, and half those amounts to the state or Indian tribe where an MRS is located;

- setting up a Nuclear Waste Negotiator office in the Executive Office of the President. . . .

TRU Waste and WIPP

The Waste Isolation Pilot Project (WIPP) in Carlsbad, New Mexico, was conceived in the early 1970s as a pilot facility for commercial high-level waste, as its name implies. It developed into a repository for military low-level waste contaminated with plutonium and other transuranic (TRU) elements, and is expected to begin receiving waste packages in 1988 or 1989. The process of siting and building the facility has yielded considerable information about the bedded salt formation in which it is located.

INTERPRETING EDITORIAL CARTOONS

This activity may be used as an individualized study guide for students in libraries and resource centers or as a discussion catalyst in small group and classroom discussions.

Although cartoons are usually humorous, the main intent of most political cartoonists is not to entertain. Cartoons express serious social comment about important issues. Using graphics and visual arts, the cartoonist expresses opinions and attitudes. By employing an entertaining and often light-hearted visual format, cartoonists may have as much or more impact on national and world issues as editorial and syndicated columnists.

Points to Consider:

1. Examine the cartoon in this activity. (See next page.)

2. How would you describe the message of this cartoon? Try to describe the message in one to three sentences.

3. Do you agree with the message expressed in this cartoon? Why or why not?

Illustration by Jerry Fearing, *St. Paul Pioneer Press-Dispatch.*

CHAPTER 2

MILITARY RADIOACTIVE WASTE

2   MILITARY RADIOACTIVE WASTE

WEAPONS COMPLEX A MASSIVE DISASTER

Radioactive Waste Campaign

*The Radioactive Waste Campaign promotes greater public aware-
ness of the dangers to human health and the biosphere from the
generation of radioactive waste. The Campaign's programs include
research, information dissemination, and public education.*

Points to Consider:

1. What was the apparent catalyst for the recent criticism of
   the bomb factories and the Department of Energy?

2. Why were workers at Rocky Flats surprised when the plant
   was closed?

3. How did the Energy Department mislead the public regarding the dangers of radioactivity exposure?

4. Describe the Department of Energy's next setback.

Jean Fazzino, "Weapons Plants Coming Apart at Seams," *RWC Waste Paper*, Winter
1988–89, pp. 3–4. Production Site Profiles excerpted from *Deadly Defense: Military
Radioactive Landfills*, a citizen guide by the Radioactive Waste Campaign.

The U.S. Department of Energy weapons production complex is an aging network of 17 facilities in 12 states. It has been plagued by environmental and safety hazards and managerial failures.

For the first time, the once ultra-secret nuclear weapons industry has had difficulty hiding behind its veil of "national security." An unprecedented deluge of publicity and criticism has been leveled at the bomb factories and the Department of Energy since last fall.

The apparent catalyst for this media blitz was the disclosure of a memorandum at a September 30, 1988, joint hearing of two Congressional committees. This memorandum came to light during an investigation of an unexplained power surge last August at one of the five production reactors at the Savannah River Plant. The memo, written on August 14, 1985 by a Du Pont supervisor at the Savannah River Plant, describes 30 "incidents of greatest significance" — including the melting of nuclear fuel — which had been kept secret for up to 31 years.

The U.S. Department of Energy weapons production complex is an aging network of 17 facilities in 12 states. It has been plagued by environmental and safety hazards and managerial failures.

Non-Stop Disclosures

Since the beginning of October, articles have appeared virtually every day in the media, notably *The New York Times,* about the nuclear weapons production complex.

Among the problems reported at Savannah River Plant (once touted as the "showcase of atomic technology") were equipment failures, massive environmental contamination and near catastrophic accidents such as a leak that deposited so much plutonium on the wall of an air duct that it nearly generated a spontaneous nuclear reaction.

Du Pont, operator of the plant, asserted that all the accidents were properly disclosed to the Department of Energy (DOE). Senator John Glenn (D-Ohio) revealed that he had repeatedly asked the Energy Department for these reports without success. Records obtained through the Freedom of Information Act in 1981 omitted the most serious accidents.

Each reactor in the complex had been shut down 9 to 12 times each year for the past two decades. Yet, the production of tritium for bombs was permitted to continue while the surrounding area was polluted.

Surprising Revelations

Within a week of the Savannah River revelations, the DOE announced a delay in the opening of the Waste Isolation Pilot Plant, the "permanent" repository for transuranic waste, in Carlsbad, New Mexico. Energy Department inspectors discovered leaks in what was supposed to be a secure repository, thus they were not satisfied that the Plant could operate safely.

A week and a half later the DOE issued an emergency order halting plutonium processing at Rocky Flats, Colorado, after three people were contaminated when they walked into a room in which plutonium-tainted equipment was being cleaned. Rocky Flats makes the first stage for new nuclear warheads and replenishes plutonium in old ones.

Workers at Rocky Flats were reportedly surprised that the Plant was closed because worse incidents in the past had not resulted in shutdowns. For example, a 1970 study following a fire recorded plutonium levels 400 to 1,500 times normal—levels greater than recorded in Nagasaki after the bomb was dropped.

The General Accounting Office revealed that the plant closing was based on far more extensive safety violations than the Energy Department had publicly acknowledged. A DOE inspector at Rocky Flats reported "significant problems in controlling radioactivity throughout the site and reports [by Rocky Flats] on environmental safety and health [were] erroneous and incomplete." However, that same inspector awarded Rockwell, the plant manager, more than $8 million in performance bonuses.

During the week following the closing of Rocky Flats, the Department of Energy acknowledged that it knew for decades that the Feed Materials Production Center in Fernald, Ohio, had exposed thousands of workers and nearby residents to uranium waste. Furthermore, *the Energy Department admitted that it had deliberately misled the public as to the dangers involved.*

Public Health at Risk

From the beginning, the government had maintained that the public need not be concerned about small amounts of radioactivity. Then on October 14, 1988, the DOE publicly acknowledged that *"any amount of radiation exposure, however small, carries with it some increased risk of adverse health effects."* Ironically, Fernald workers are now required to pay more of their own medical insurance costs!

Residents near the plant had been reassured since 1951 that emissions were so slight as to be harmless. In those 37 years the plant has dumped 13 million pounds of uranium into waste pits, 170,000 pounds into the Great Miami Aquifer and almost 300,000 pounds into the air. The Energy Department is still unsure about the exact figures.

Two days later (on October 16), Congress budgeted the Centers for Disease Control to do a health study of local residents near the Hanford Plant. This plant, near Richland, Washington, produced plutonium for the bomb that destroyed Nagasaki.

Documents show that in the zeal to make bombs, plant managers allowed releases because they believed that Hanford's mission to defend the nation's security outweighed dangers to the public. According to an October 17, 1988, article in *The New York Times,* some experts estimate that families living downwind received radiation doses 10 times those of Chernobyl residents. Cleaning up the pollution caused by 45 years of plutonium production at Hanford is expected to cost more than $50 billion.

Another Setback

In an incident reminiscent of the wandering garbage barge, the Department of Energy was dealt its next setback. Idaho Governor Cecil Andrus, a strong supporter of the nuclear weapons program, stopped at the border a red railroad boxcar laden with waste from Rocky Flats.

In announcing his decision, Andrus said the people of Idaho "were tired of being good citizens." In 1970, the Atomic Energy

23

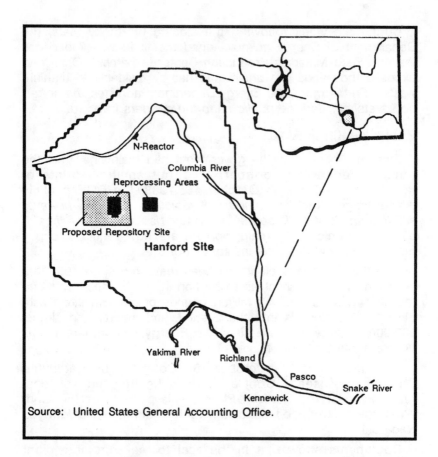

Source: United States General Accounting Office.

Commission promised Idaho that the Rocky Flats waste would be gone in 10 years. But when the opening of the Waste Isolation Pilot Plant was postponed, it became more apparent that the storage was becoming permanent.

Meanwhile, back at Rocky Flats, Colorado, the waste was accumulating with nowhere to go. At full operation, the plant produces a boxcar of waste each week. Colorado Governor Roy Romer declared he would not allow long-term storage at Rocky Flats. . . .

Sixteen of the nuclear weapons production sites were described as having very serious pollution problems. The 17th site—the Waste Isolation Pilot Plant— has not opened yet. . . .

Production Site Profiles

Hanford Reservation

The Hanford Site is located in semi-arid southeastern

24

Washington, 20 miles from the Yakima Reservation. Richland, Pasco, and Kennewick (the Tri-Cities area, pop. 140,000) are situated nearby downtown on the Columbia River. Portland, Oregon (pop. 360,000) is about 230 miles downstream. Since its inception, Hanford has produced plutonium for nuclear weapons. As a result, a large amount of radioactive waste has been generated. Billions of gallons of contaminated water have been poured into seepage beds, resulting in a surface plume of tritium which has moved six miles to the Columbia River. A deep underground aquifer has been contaminated with iodine-129. Over 500,000 gallons of high-level radioactive waste have leaked from tanks.

Idaho National Engineering Laboratory (INEL)

INEL is located in southeastern Idaho, 22 miles west of Idaho Falls. INEL sits on the Snake River Plain, recharge area for the Snake River Aquifer. Sixteen billion gallons of waste water containing 70,000 curies of radioactivity have been dumped into the Snake River Aquifer, which discharges into the Snake River, which flows into the Columbia River near Hanford. At INEL, enriched uranium is separated from irradiated naval and experimental reactor fuel, which is shipped by rail from ocean ports. The radioactive landfill itself is 140 acres, containing plutonium-contaminated waste from Rocky Flats [another production site located at Golden, Colorado].

Lawrence Livermore National Laboratory and Sandia National Laboratory Livermore

The labs are located in the Livermore Valley three miles east of Livermore (pop. 50,000) and 40 miles east of San Francisco (pop. 700,000). The city of Tracy (pop. 25,000) is located six miles northeast of Site 300, where high explosives are tested. The primary mission of Lawrence Livermore National Laboratory at Livermore develops new warhead components and at the Nevada Test Site puts the entire new warhead together for testing. The labs sit above an important aquifer for the Livermore Valley. Site 300 is leaking tritium into groundwater beyond the site boundary and above state limits. Uranium and tritium are dispersed during open air testing.

Los Alamos National Laboratory

Los Alamos National Laboratory is located 25 miles northwest of Santa Fe and 60 miles north of Albuquerque, New Mexico. There are 170,000 inhabitants within a 50-mile radius. The lab sits on a plateau between a mountain range to the west and a valley to the east. Los Alamos continues to be the major design center for nuclear warheads. . . .

Mound Laboratory

Mound Laboratory sits atop the Great Miami Aquifer and adjacent to the Great Miami River, 10 miles southwest of Dayton in Miamisburg, Ohio. About 3,400,000 people live within 50 miles of the plant, including residents of Cincinnati. Mound Laboratory produces detonators for activating explosives in nuclear warheads, recovers tritium from weapons components, and constructs plutonium heat generators for satellites. Accidents and radioactive leakage at Mound have contaminated workers, vast areas of the site, and adjacent public ponds and park land. Tritium and plutonium are contained in sediments of the Old Erie Canal.

Nevada Test Site

The Nevada Test Site is located 65 miles northwest of Las Vegas, and roughly 20 miles east of the California border. Nuclear weapons are assembled and tested at the site. Through 1987, about 100 atmospheric and almost 600 underground tests have taken place. The site also serves as a waste disposal facility for other nuclear weapons sites. Underground tests have released enormous quantities of radioactive material at or near a major underground aquifer. The soil is heavily contaminated with plutonium and other radionuclides from above ground tests and breakthrough of underground tests.

Oak Ridge Gaseous Diffusion Plant

The Gaseous Diffusion Plant is in the eastern part of Tennessee, about 15 miles west of Knoxville (pop. 183,000). There are about 680,000 people who live within a 50-mile radius of the plant. With little likelihood it will be re-opened, the Gaseous Diffusion Plant now serves as a waste dump for the Y-12 Plant and the Oak Ridge National Laboratory. Holding ponds and burial grounds contain up to 124,000 pounds of uranium. During its operation, 36,000 pounds of uranium were released to water and 23,000 pounds to air. Large quantities of water-soluble technetium-99 are contained within piping.

Paducah Gaseous Diffusion Plant

The Paducah Gaseous Diffusion Plant is located 11 miles west of Paducah (pop. 35,000) and about three miles south of the Ohio River and the Illinois border in western Kentucky. The Paducah Plant enriches uranium for use in the Portsmouth Gaseous Diffusion Plant and the Hanford plutonium production reactor (via Fernald). Since 1952, over seven million pounds of uranium have been buried on site, 60,000 pounds have been released into local creeks, and 130,000 pounds into the atmosphere.

Pantex Plant

The Pantex Plant is located in Carson County in the Texas Panhandle, 17 miles northeast of downtown Amarillo (pop. 150,000). The principal operation performed at Pantax is the assembly and disassembly of nuclear weapons. . . .

Portsmouth Uranium Enrichment Complex

The Portsmouth Uranium Enrichment Complex is located two miles south of Piketon and 16 miles north of Portsmouth, Ohio, in the south central part of the state. The Ohio-Kentucky border and the Ohio River are 20 miles south of the plant. The function of the plant is to enrich the uranium up to 4 percent uranium-235 for use in commercial nuclear power reactors, and nuclear warheads. Since 1954, over 11,000 pounds of uranium have been buried on-site, 17,000 pounds dumped into local streams, and 23,000 pounds released into the atmosphere.

Rocky Flats Plant

The Rocky Flats Plant is located at Golden, Colorado, 16 miles northwest of downtown Denver. Almost 2 million persons live within 30 miles of the plant, whose primary function in the weapons complex is to produce plutonium triggers for nuclear warheads. With the cessation of plutonium production at Hanford's N-reactor, and the reduction in power levels at the Savannah River Plant reactors since the Chernobyl accident, recycling of nuclear warheads at the plant has become the major means of providing plutonium for new warheads. Fires at the plant have distributed a large amount of plutonium into the air, soil, and water supplies.

Sandia National Laboratory

Sandia National Laboratory is located immediately south of Albuquerque (pop. 330,000), within the boundaries of the Kirtland Air Force Base. . . .Sandia designs and tests the arming, fusing, and firing system used in nuclear warheads and bombs, and does research on X-ray lasers for the proposed "Star Wars" system. . . .

Savannah River Plant

The Savannah River Plant is located next to the Savannah River, 13 miles south of Aiken, South Carolina (pop. 15,000) and 20 miles southeast of Augusta, Georgia (pop. 50,000). The Savannah River Plant produces plutonium-239 and tritium, for nuclear weapons. The Plant contains three nuclear reactors operating at reduced capacity, and two reprocessing plants to chemically separate plutonium, tritium and other nuclear materials. The site has enormous quantities of nuclear waste in landfills, seepage basins and 51 underground tanks. About 30 million gallons of radioactive effluent are discharged annually into seepage basins. Substantial leaching of the burial grounds and surface impoundments is causing severe contamination of the shallow aquifers and groundwater, thus endangering the Tuscaloosa aquifer used by Atlanta. The aquifer is already contaminated by toxic chemicals from the plant.

3   MILITARY RADIOACTIVE WASTE

RESPONSIBLE MANAGEMENT OF NUCLEAR PRODUCTION PLANTS

J. James Exon

J. James Exon testified in his capacity as chairman of the Subcommittee on Strategic Forces and Nuclear Deterrence.

Points to Consider:

1. Describe the Energy Department's safety record.

2. Why is the author concerned about the age of the DOE's facilities?

3. How did the DOE respond to the recommendations in the GAO reports?

4. What is the author's overall opinion of the DOE?

Excerpted from the *Congressional Record* (Senate), March 18, 1988, pp. S2537-S2538.

Let me simply say that we cannot characterize DOE as willing to sacrifice health, safety, and environment to the god of production.

A Fine Safety Record

We all know that the aging of our critical nuclear production facilities does increase the risk of a nuclear accident or incident. But what exactly is the Energy Department's record in the safety area? Let me quote from the subcommittee's report:

> However one chooses to examine the record — reactor incidents, day-to-day operation, worker radiation exposure, or worker injury rates — the Department of Energy's safety record has been excellent.

Witnesses from the National Academy of Sciences and the Occupational Safety and Health Administration all testified that the Energy Department's record is as good or, in most cases, substantially better than comparable commercial sector figures and well above minimum safety requirements.

Some Problems

This is good news. However, I do agree that risk always exists and we dare not become complacent. I am especially worried that the Department of Energy (DOE) has allowed its facilities to age to the point that concerns about both safety and production to meet defense needs have grown to major proportions.

Compounding the problem is the frequent confusion between the issue of production safety and the very serious environmental waste problem.

I have been disappointed with the lack of progress made toward replacing these aging facilities and the cleanup of contaminated sites. I have been pressing for new facilities as soon as possible so that our security needs will continue to be met. I have also pressed for action to clean up sites. But production safety and cleanup are two distinct issues.

The environmental restoration is relevant to the production safety issue in this one respect. It is an issue, like facilities modernization, that has been ignored for too long.

Monitoring Nuclear Weapons Production

Until this modernization occurs, we are going to have to watch our existing facilities very carefully. And I tell all my

ACTIONS BEING TAKEN

Since 1986, under the direction of Secretary John S. Herrington, the Department of Energy (DOE) has been conducting a series of intensive reviews of the safety of its nuclear facilities. In addition to reviews and appraisals performed by the department and expert consultants, the Secretary requested that the National Academy of Sciences conduct a detailed study of the department's reactors, including the three production reactors at Savannah River. The reports from all of these reviews have been made public.

As a result of the department's safety initiative, a number of issues were identified involving the Savannah River reactors. The DOE has made a firm commitment to resolve all of the issues raised. In addition, the Department has announced its intention to replace the three Savannah River reactors, which were built in the 1950s, with new production reactors expected to be built at Savannah River and at the Idaho National Engineering Laboratory.

Excerpted from the Congressional Record (Senate), October 19, 1988, p. S6809

colleagues this is going to be very expensive—much more than DOE can afford from its current budget levels. I have been monitoring the nuclear weapons production base and will continue to do this. Last month, we learned about a major dispute between the Energy Department and the contractor at the Savannah River Plant's L-reactor.

Supposedly, a contractor threatened to quit over DOE's opposition to taking necessary safety actions. I immediately held a hearing of the Strategic Subcommittee to look into this matter. What we learned from both the contractor and the Energy Department laid to rest the alleged irresponsibility on the Department's behalf. Through the Subcommittee on Strategic Forces and Nuclear Deterrence, I intend to continue my monitoring of this particular matter and the nuclear production complex. . . .

The Armed Services Committee has never failed to produce a defense authorization bill and I see nothing to preclude passage of one again this year. In fact, the Armed Services Committee has already completed much of its work on this particular bill and we should see its passage soon.

Indeed, regardless of what happens here today, I intend to have legislation regarding oversight of the nuclear weapons complex included in the defense authorization bill. I will certainly fight for inclusion of such legislation in conference with the House should that be necessary. . . .

GAO Reports

There is one other matter that I must touch on briefly. I must correct what I regard as a serious misimpression that the distinguished Senator from Ohio [Senator Metzenbaum] inevitably leaves behind when he addresses the General Accounting Office (GAO) studies of the Department of Energy's supposed sins in this area.

The senior Senator from Ohio has made a point by bringing a stack of GAO reports with him to all of our Armed Services Committee meetings on DOE oversight. I can almost cite the color of the page because I have seen them so very often.

But let me make it clear, the Senator is to be commended for his diligence in examining the issue where DOE's prior performance has been less than stellar and for his use of the GAO as an investigating tool.

What he omits to do as he waves his stack of GAO reports at us and talks about the dangers of Chernobyl, which are real, is to give the Department of Energy any credit for having reviewed and implemented most or all of the GAO recommendations.

The DOE's Response

Earlier this month, I asked the Department of Energy to review every one of these 21 reports, to dig out every major recommendation in them and report to me what the Department of Energy has done or is doing to implement these recommendations.

I also asked them to highlight any GAO recommendations with which they do not agree. . . .

Let me tell you about their response to those 21 GAO reports, those reports we have seen so often — reports, by the way, which date way back to January 1979. Some of them are nearly 10 years old.

Of the 21 GAO reports that the Senator waves in evidence, seven of them or one-third of the total are merely reports on various subjects which contain no major recommendations for

32

DOE action.

One additional report contained only recommendations for congressional action, not recommendation by DOE or action necessary by DOE. Of the remaining 13 GAO reports that the Senator has stacked before him, nine of those reports contain recommendations with which the DOE is concerned, has acted on and implemented and for which the DOE should be given some credit for constructive action.

In other words, nine of those reports are history. They identified problems and made recommendations and DOE has completed corrective action. Thus, there are only two major recommendations that are outstanding, for which the Department of Energy cannot forecast a timetable for implementation even though it concurred with those GAO recommendations as well.

DOE: Diligent and Responsive

In clarifying this record, I wish to again make clear that both GAO and the Senator from Ohio have performed a useful service in highlighting major problems of health, safety, and environment at DOE facilities. I also wish to be clear that I do not intend my remarks to absolve DOE of blame or responsibility for permitting the conditions that GAO found in their reports to develop in the first place. But I do believe DOE has made a major effort to be both diligent and responsive when problems have been identified, and the distinguished Senator from Ohio gives them no credit whatsoever for that diligence and responsiveness. Instead, he brandishes that huge stack of GAO reports as though they constitute a set of current-day horror stories that DOE is unwilling to address, unless we in the Congress whip them into line. I submit that that is not the case at DOE and has not been for some years. Many of the problems DOE faces are inherited problems that date from the days when "safe disposal" meant digging a hole in the ground somewhere well away from the plant and dumping stuff into it. Obviously, DOE doesn't operate that way any longer, but those old problems are still there. And the only thing that will fix those problems is money, money, and more money – not oversight, oversight, and more oversight.

Substantial Credit Is Due

In closing, let me simply say that we cannot characterize DOE as willing to sacrifice health, safety, and environment to the god of production, as my friend from Ohio sometimes seems to suggest when his evangelical streak takes hold. If the Secretary of Energy cannot be counted on to balance environmental health and safety issues against production needs, then neither can the secretary of any other department be trusted to balance diverse and conflicting objectives. Worse yet, we could not count on inspectors general—which this Congress has created in abundance—to do their jobs, since they report to departmental secretaries. We could not expect the Defense Contract Audit Service to reliably uncover contract fraud and abuse, since that might jeopardize the production of military hardware, and so forth. So, let us give credit where credit is due, and in this case, substantial credit is due the Department of Energy for responding vigorously and forthrightly to GAO recommendations, to the point where only a handful of recommendations are outstanding. Let us stop waving old reports as though nothing has happened since the reports were issued.

4 MILITARY RADIOACTIVE WASTE

THE PILOT WASTE DUMP IS NEARLY READY FOR USE

Jill Lytle

Jill Lytle testified in her capacity as deputy assistant secretary for Nuclear Materials of the United States Department of Energy.

Points to Consider:

1. What kind of waste will be stored at the Waste Isolation Pilot Plant (WIPP)?

2. How is transuranic (TRU) waste defined?

3. What extensive tests will take place and for what purpose?

4. Why will WIPP be safe to operate?

Excerpted from the testimony of Jill Lytle before the House Subcommittee of the Committee on Government Operations, September 13, 1988.

Construction of WIPP is essentially complete. Our objective is to begin the demonstration phase as soon as all safety-related appraisals are complete and environmental requirements are met. We anticipate all of these requirements could be satisfied in the next few months.

The Waste Isolation Pilot Plant (WIPP) has been one of the Department of Energy's (DOE) most important projects. Given the national importance of nuclear waste disposal, successful operation of WIPP is vital. WIPP is very close to being ready to start its demonstration phase.

Prior to startup of this facility, of course, we must assure that all safety and environmental requirements have been met. We believe we can do that and be ready to start by the end of this year. All construction needed to open and operate the facility is complete. This includes buildings, waste handling equipment, and underground placement rooms. The personnel are trained and ready.

We have conducted successful demonstrations of both emplacement and retrieval operations. Of more than 16,000 items necessary to start actual operations, fewer than 200 remain to be completed at this time.

Extensive preoperational readiness reviews are being conducted at the site and an independent review will be conducted by our Headquarters Safety Oversight Office.

As the project progressed, great attention was paid to ensure that this facility was built to meet the highest safety standards. This is described in a safety analysis report, which has been reviewed by both the State of New Mexico and our Headquarters Safety Oversight Office. We expect the final version of this report to be completed in October. . . .

We are currently urging the passage of legislation to withdraw permanently the WIPP site from the public land laws and to transfer control of the site to the Secretary of Energy. I would like to provide some background on the project's history and status of current and planned activities.

Background

In 1979 WIPP was authorized by Public Law 96-164 to demonstrate the safe disposal of radioactive wastes resulting from the defense activities and programs of the United States exempted from regulation by the Nuclear Regulatory Commission (NRC). Since the early 1940s, the United States has been generating radioactive waste in national defense programs through the production of nuclear weapons and the operation of military reactors. This waste is currently being stored at government sites around the country. DOE is responsible for developing and implementing methods for the safe and environmentally acceptable disposal of this waste.

The waste bound for WIPP is known as transuranic (TRU) waste. TRU waste is any solid waste, other than high-level waste or spent nuclear fuel, that is contaminated with nuclides heavier than uranium to such an extent as to require permanent isolation from the accessible environment. TRU waste is generated in a variety of physical forms, ranging from unprocessed general trash such as absorbent papers and protecting clothing to decommissioned equipment and glove boxes.

The TRU waste will be stored at WIPP in a 100-acre storage area at a depth of 2,150 feet beneath the surface in a deep bedded salt formation. In addition, this area will contain the underground support facilities and the experimental area. The WIPP surface facilities accommodate the personnel, equipment, and support services required for the receipt, preparation, and transfer of waste from the surface to the underground. The surface facilities are located on an area of approximately 35 acres.

The WIPP land area is a square totaling 16 square miles in size. The inner four sections of land constitute the outer boundaries of excavation for the underground development. The outer 12 sections provide an approximate one mile subsurface natural barrier for the waste emplaced in WIPP. This buffer zone is an integral part of the disposal system. The Department is negotiating for the purchase of the last of the outstanding mineral leases on the WIPP land area.

A Phased Project

WIPP is a phased project. The Final Environmental Impact Statement (EIS) for the project was issued in October 1980. The Record of Decision to proceed with the project was issued in January 1981. Shortly thereafter, in April 1981, activity began on the Site and Preliminary Design Validation (SPDV) phase of the project which provided valuable, detailed knowledge of the subsurface conditions. Extensive surface-based geologic and hydraulic studies have been made at the WIPP site since 1973. . . .

Upon completion of the SPDV phase in 1983, DOE determined that construction of the WIPP could proceed in a safe and environmentally acceptable manner. This initial baseline construction, managed by the U.S. Army Corps of Engineers, was completed in Fiscal Year 1987. Additional construction or modifications which were identified during operational reviews, such as a ventilation shaft, Safety and Emergency Services Building, and construction and salt handling hoist upgrade are managed by Westinghouse, the management and operating contractor.

The total project cost for WIPP is $700 million. . . . Our objective is to have the facility ready for operation in the first quarter of Fiscal Year 1989.

Extensive Testing

An extensive experimental test program will be conducted to

SCHEDULE FOR THE REPOSITORY

2003	Begin Receiving Spent Fuel and High-Level Waste at the Repository
1998	Start Repository Construction
1995	Submit License Application to Nuclear Regulatory Commission
1994	Environmental Impact Statement
DECEMBER 1988	Site Characterization Plan
DECEMBER 1987	Yucca Mountain Designated by Congress as Candidate Site
1982	Nuclear Waste Policy Act

Source: Department of Energy.

provide data for: (1) validation of repository design (shaft and waste room plugging and sealing and engineered barriers), and (2) determination of compliance with environmental requirements for a waste disposal facility.

An equally important operational test will be conducted to demonstrate the handling, certification, and transportation aspects of the entire waste disposal system as well as its ability to comply with Resource Conservation and Recovery Act (RCRA) requirements, NRC and Department of Transportation (DOT) transportation requirements and Environmental Protection Agency (EPA) standards covering the operational phase of a disposal facility.

It is DOE's view that this operational test will be most effective as a demonstration of waste disposal as directed by Public Law 96-164 if it is conducted at near full-scale receipt rates. DOE estimates that this will require emplacement of up to 15 percent of the repository's capacity (approximately 125,000 55-gallon drums). The waste will be stored in a fully retrievable manner and in a way to facilitate the addition of backfill at a later date. . . .

The final phase, operation of the repository, will begin once the decision has been made regarding permanent disposal of the waste. The anticipated operating life is 25 years. The backlog of TRU waste now stored at several DOE sites around the country will be eliminated. . . .

Safety at WIPP

A comprehensive industrial safety program is in place for worker protection. This program includes extensive safety training for underground employees. Also, during construction, particular attention was paid to the quality of workmanship, through a quality assurance program, to ensure that critical components were built properly and will operate as planned.

To protect the residents of Carlsbad and WIPP employees, WIPP safety personnel have developed and implemented effective strategies for dealing with potential emergency situations, for example, tornadoes, floods, and fires. WIPP is equipped with fire trucks for both the surface and underground facilities and has an underground ambulance. On a regular basis, the WIPP emergency team conducts drills with neighboring organizations, such as surrounding fire departments. . . .

Conclusion

Construction of WIPP is essentially complete. Our objective is to begin the demonstration phase as soon as all safety-related appraisals are complete and environmental requirements are met. We anticipate all of these requirements could be satisfied in the next few months.

5 MILITARY RADIOACTIVE WASTE

THE PILOT WASTE DUMP IS ALREADY IN TROUBLE

Robyn Seydel

Robyn Seydel wrote this article as a special to the Guardian. *The* Guardian *describes itself as a weekly independent radical newspaper.*

Points to Consider:

1. What is the purpose of the Waste Isolation Pilot Plant (WIPP)?

2. How do critics describe problems surrounding WIPP?

3. What kind of wastes will be stored in WIPP?

4. Describe the Land Withdrawal Bill.

Robyn Seydel, "Pilot Waste Dump Is Already in Trouble," *Guardian*, October 12, 1988.

Activists continue to believe that due to geologic problems at the site and transportation safety issues, WIPP will never be safe.

Safety issues at the nation's first permanent nuclear waste dump, the Waste Isolation Pilot Plant, or WIPP, have stalled its opening from October 1 to some time in early 1989. At a congressional hearing on September 13, Representative Mike Sinar (D-Okla.), made public internal Department of Energy (DOE) memos that reveal that safety experts within the agency itself do not believe "adequate documentation" of the facility's design and construction have been provided.

Design and Construction Problems

The WIPP site is a military nuclear waste dump in the desert, some 20 miles east of Carlsbad, New Mexico. It consists of a series of tunnels, corridors, ventilation shafts and storage rooms, constructed 2,150 feet below the surface at a cost of $700 million. It is situated in a supposedly dry salt bed, but brine is seeping through the walls and floors. Scientists at the National Academy of Sciences have expressed concern about the leaks. Geologist Roger Anderson of the University of New Mexico says it is possible the water and waste could form a radioactive slurry which, during the 250,000 years the wastes must be contained, could come to the surface, as the resources of this mineral- and oil-rich area become more important and drilling occurs.

The DOE was embarrassed by the memos brought to light by Sinar. "They [the DOE] were frantic all day in efforts to find ways to cover themselves," Representative Bill Richardson (D-N.M.) told a local newspaper.

In early August engineers and scientists from Brookhaven National Laboratories and the DOE visited the site for a final safety analysis, and learned that on June 24 a joint on a pipe used in the fire control system had ruptured, causing $100,000 to $200,000 worth of damage. Facility managers in Carlsbad could not provide documentation assuring the ventilation shafts, elevator shafts, fire prevention systems, electrical circuits, waste handling and other systems were built and were functioning properly.

At the Washington hearing, plant managers also revealed that the majority of wastes shipped to WIPP will be "mixed wastes," a combination of radioactive and hazardous wastes. This classification includes many carcinogens and other chemicals known to destroy liver, kidney, bone, heart, central nervous system and respiratory system tissues.

'Mixed Wastes'

Mixed wastes come under the stringent, 12-year-old Resource Conservation and Recovery Act, which mandates that they be disposed of in a licensed facility. It may take as long as two years to license WIPP. A series of DOE applications and state and federal exemptions that could allow WIPP to open sooner have environmentalists up in arms. Dan Reicher, an attorney with the National Resources Defense Council in Washington, D.C., says a lawsuit is "a very real possibility."

Environmental groups have long been opposed to WIPP, and as the proposed opening of the controversial dump nears, new groups have joined in the struggle. The Committee to Make WIPP Safe was recently formed to being in more moderate views. In Santa Fe, Concerned Citizens for Nuclear Safety have gotten the Santa Fe Public School System to send home a letter with every child protesting DOE's nuclear-waste truck routes along the busiest streets, where many schools are located and children walk daily. Parents and citizens statewide have raised a public outcry, which resulted in the largest demonstration ever seen in Santa Fe, on July 16, as well as ongoing activism. Business groups have bought air time on the radio and space in newspapers, and have utilized their main street display windows to educate people about the dangers involved.

Cartoon by Jeff MacNelly. Reprinted by permission: Tribune Media Services.

Safety

Anti-WIPP activists continue to believe that due to geologic problems at the site and transportation safety issues, WIPP will never be safe. Events surrounding the Tru-Pac container, specially designed for the transport of waste destined for WIPP, seem to prove the point. Having failed its safety test in 1984, the DOE applied to the Department of Transportation (DOT) for a waiver to use the container anyway. The DOT refused, and the redesigned Tru-Pac II failed its puncture test in August. Although redesign, testing, and the NRC certification process may take as long as a year, DOE officials plan to go ahead with transportation of wastes anyway, using other containers.

Land Withdrawal Bill

The fight over the Land Withdrawal Bill, which has been moving slowly through Congress since last March, is still a major obstacle to WIPP's opening. The bill would allow the 10,240-acre WIPP area to be transferred from public use to DOE jurisdiction. Although New Mexican representatives admit they have received more letters and calls opposing the Withdrawal Bill than on all other issues combined, they continue to push it.

EPA Standards

Part of the controversy surrounding the bill stems from differences in opinions on whether or not WIPP must meet Environmental Protection Agency (EPA) standards before waste goes in. The Richardson-Udall House version, still in subcommittee, requires that EPA standards be met. The Senate version, which has made it to the floor, allows the DOE to dump 25,000 barrels of waste before it must show it can meet standards some five years down the road.

For its part, the DOE is threatening administrative takeover of the land, which would deprive the state of New Mexico of $250,000,000 for city bypass and new roads and mineral rights. The Southwest Research and Information Center and others say that if administrative withdrawal goes through, the DOE will be faced with yet another lawsuit.

6 MILITARY RADIOACTIVE WASTE

MEETING NATIONAL SECURITY NEEDS

Theodore J. Garrish

Theodore J. Garrish testified in his capacity as assistant secretary for nuclear energy of the United States Department of Energy.

Points to Consider:

1. Why does the United States need to maintain a uranium enrichment capability?

2. What kind of problems are facing the uranium enrichment and uranium mining industries?

3. Describe the structural changes that are needed to improve the uranium enrichment enterprise.

4. What benefits would be derived from a comprehensive uranium revitalization proposal?

Excerpted from the testimony of Theodore J. Garrish before the House Subcommittee on Energy and the Environment of the House Committee on Interior and Insular Affairs, June 28, 1988.

A comprehensive uranium revitalization proposal would help strengthen national security and energy security.

The Department of Energy (DOE) has endeavored to manage the uranium enrichment enterprise in the most professional, businesslike manner possible. Our objective is to provide a stable, reliable supply of enrichment services to meet energy and national security needs. To the extent possible under existing authority, we have offered flexible contract terms and prices while continuing to meet our legal mandate to recover the government costs. We have retired unneeded facilities, focused our research and development efforts, and increased sales. Our overall objective has been and continues to be to make the enrichment enterprise as healthy and robust as possible.

The Need for Uranium Enrichment

Energy security and national security provide strong motivation for maintaining an efficient, stable, and economically competitive uranium enrichment capability in the United States. Nuclear power contributes one-sixth of our nation's electric power and is an important part of ensuring that Americans will have an adequate and reliable supply of electricity now and in the future. This supply of electricity and the domestic employment it ensures require a secure, reliable, and economical supply of enriched uranium—free of the threat of foreign supply disruptions or price controls. In addition, foreign commercial sales of enriched uranium amounting to about $500 million each year aid in the nation's balance of trade payments and contribute to the nation's nuclear nonproliferation efforts through our involvement in the nuclear fuel cycle of foreign countries. Finally, important national security objectives are supported by the availability of a secure, dependable supply of highly enriched uranium at reasonable costs for U.S. naval forces and other defense programs. . . .

Both the uranium enrichment and uranium mining industries face serious problems today. Both face strong foreign competition; both are experiencing financial and economic hardships as a result of reduced demand; and the enrichment enterprise is encumbered by the sluggishness and inflexibility of government bureaucracy.

The needs are clear. The enrichment enterprise needs to be run in a more businesslike, profitable manner, with flexibilities characteristic of a private business. To compete more effectively, the enterprise needs market-based contract terms and prices, and continued minimization of long-term operational costs. In addition, it must promote future competitiveness through efficient development of the laser enrichment process. The miners need a healthier, more robust industry through increased demand for domestic uranium. Moreover, an equitable way of allocating the burden of mill tailings remedial actions among the beneficiaries of past production is needed.

Uranium Enrichment Structural Changes

One of the goals of the Administration is to transfer to the private sector those government functions that can best be performed by the private sector. The uranium enrichment enterprise has all of the key commercial characteristics for privatization. At this time, the Executive Branch is prohibited from studying or proposing privatization for the enrichment business. However, based on previous studies, the Administration continues to believe that the uranium enrichment enterprise should be restructured as a more commercially oriented entity.

To accomplish an effective transition from a government-managed program to a private sector organization, the uranium enrichment business, first and foremost, must be healthy, profitable, and well managed. A major step in this direction would be to establish the enterprise as a wholly-owned government corporation. Such an entity, with a corporate-like structure, stock held by the Treasury, and increased flexibility in marketing, contracting, management, and administration could begin the process of establishing a more stable, viable, commercially attractive business. Operation in this mode would also provide time to prepare for the transition to full privatization by addressing issues such as Nuclear Regulatory Commission licensing. In the future, stock could be sold to the private sector as was done with Conrail, and a private corporation established. The issuance of stock, reflecting the government's investment in the enrichment enterprise, and its eventual sale can serve as an effective vehicle to ultimately privatize this enrichment enterprise. This could offer an opportunity to maximize the return on the government's investment. . . .

The Benefits of Revitalization

The benefits of such a comprehensive uranium revitalization proposal include:

- Strengthens national security and energy security of the United States.
- Reinforces free trade principles of the Free Trade Agreement by eliminating import restrictions.
- Provides system to enable mill tailings cleanup with corresponding environmental benefits.
- Provides the opportunity for lower nuclear fuel costs to utilities, which could be passed through as rate decreases to ratepayers.
- Resolves longstanding contentious issue with miners, utilities, and DOE.

If comprehensive uranium legislation now being considered is modified along the lines suggested above and approved, it will definitely enhance the viability of those two key nuclear industries. A comprehensive uranium bill would help ensure a strong sales base and provide the basis for financially strong companies in the uranium enrichment and uranium mining and milling industries. One benefit of the comprehensive legislative remedy would be increased pricing flexibility for the uranium enrichment enterprise to meet foreign competition, or to provide substantial dividends to the U.S. Treasury at current prices. It could also provide the opportunity for lower nuclear fuel costs to utilities, which could be passed through as rate decreases to ratepayers. Finally, a system to enable mill tailings cleanup with

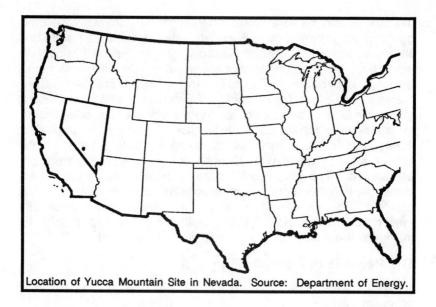

Location of Yucca Mountain Site in Nevada. Source: Department of Energy.

corresponding environmental benefits could effectively solve a longstanding impediment to the viability of the U.S. mining industry. The net effect of these benefits would help strengthen the national and energy security of the United States.

Legislation that both restructures the U.S. enrichment enterprise and revitalizes the U.S. mining industry is highly desirable. Restructuring the enrichment enterprise as a government-owned stock corporation is needed to enhance the competitive position of this important national industry. A legislative remedy to foster the health and vitality of the U.S. uranium industry is also highly desirable. Alternatives to promote both the U.S. uranium and enrichment industries should be vigorously pursued, and timely, decisive action by the Congress is needed for this purpose. We are eager to work with Congress to refine details as necessary to complete this important action.

MILITARY RADIOACTIVE WASTE

THE URANIUM INDUSTRY: RADIATING TRIBAL LANDS

Akwesasne Notes

The following reading, by Tom Barry, appeared in Akwesasne Notes — *the official publication of the Mohawk Nation at Akwesasne near Roosevelt, New York.*

Points to Consider:

1. Where does much of the nation's uranium mining and milling occur?

2. How has radioactive exposure affected Navajo uranium miners?

3. Why are U.S. companies interested in aboriginal land in Australia?

4. Define the "apocalyptic generation."

Tom Barry, "Land Rights, Not Uranium Mines," *Akwesasne Notes*, mid-winter 1989, p. 15.

Sickness, death, and destruction caused by nuclear power development is already a severe reality for many Indian people of the Southwest.

Native Americans stand at the front of the hazardous nuclear fuel process. Much of the nation's uranium mining and milling occurs on Indian land in New Mexico, Arizona, Wyoming, South Dakota, and Washington. Thousands of Indians work in the radioactive conditions of the underground uranium mines, and many have already died of radiation-induced lung cancer.

Uranium Mining in New Mexico

On April 28 and 29, about 500 Indian, Chicano, and white people rallied in front of Gulf Oil's uranium mine on Mount Taylor in northwestern New Mexico. They gathered from all parts of the country to demand an immediate halt to uranium mining on Indian land and the shutdown of the nuclear power industry. The demonstration was organized by the American Indian Environmental Council (AIEC) following the national No Nuclear Strategy Conference in Kentucky last August.

New Mexico is the nation's largest uranium producing state, with over half of the production of this radioactive fuel coming from Navajo and Pueblo Indian land. Gulf Oil is sinking the world's deepest uranium mine shaft into the side of Mount Taylor, a mountain considered sacred by the Indians of northwestern New Mexico. The Gulf site also sits next to a rural Chicano town on lands stolen from the town's community land grant.

While Indians and Chicanos were calling for land rights, the nearby uranium boomtown of Grants, New Mexico was hosting a parade to promote nuclear energy. Grants bills itself as "the Uranium Capitol of the World." The Energy Association of Taxpayers (EAT), an organization supported by the uranium industry, sponsored the march. The industry and many residents of the Grants area feel threatened by the efforts of Indians and anti-nuclear activists to shut down the nuclear industry. EAT recently formed after a group of 92 Navajos sued the Department of Interior and the Department of Energy to stop uranium mining until adequate environmental safeguards are found for radioactivity released during the extraction and processing of the ore.

A Severe Reality for Indian People

The Department of Interior calls northwestern New Mexico

WORST RADIOACTIVE WASTE SPILL

The United Nuclear Corporation (UNC) bought the land near the small Navajo village of Church Rock during the peak of uranium mining, in 1969. . . .

While the Navajos debated amongst themselves the impact of the mining near their communities, the United Nuclear Corporation finished building a dam that they claimed would hold back tons of radioactive waste and water left over from the milling process.

Just before dawn on July 16, the United Nuclear dam broke with a force that sounded like a thunder clap. Tons of radioactive waste rushed down the winding Puerco River past Navajo homes, the city of Gallup, the Navajo village of Manuelito, the small community of Sanders, Arizona, and Petrified Forest National Park—a distance of 120 miles.

Ninety-four million gallons of radioactive water and 1,100 tons of radioactive rock emptied into the Puerco River, contaminating the land with lead, polonium, and cancer-causing thorium. The incident is still considered the largest radioactive spill in the history of the United States. . .

The accident never became a household word like Three Mile Island. The national media virtually ignored it.

Colleen Keane, "The Legend of the Rock," Earth Island Journal, *Fall 1988*

"the hottest uranium exploration area in the country." The largest open pit uranium mine in the world operates on the Laguna Pueblo on the eastern side of Mount Taylor.

"Because over 55 percent of the nation's uranium is on Indian land, we're the first to be poisoned," declared Diane Ortiz from the Acoma Pueblo.

"Indian people," she said, "have always had a deep respect for nature. We did not try to control it, manipulate it, or use it for destructive purposes. Uranium mining is an insult to the health of all living things. It should be left in the ground; America doesn't need it."

Sickness, death, and destruction caused by nuclear power development is already a severe reality for many Indian people of the Southwest. Due to their high level of radioactive exposure, at least 25 Navajo uranium miners have died of lung cancer and another 20 have developed the dread disease in the Shiprock area of the Navajo Nation. A total of ten million tons of radioactive uranium wastes lies unattended near Navajo communities. Several communities — never warned of the hazard — have constructed their homes from the radioactive mill tailings.

The Booming Industry

The increased price of uranium in the past four years has increased uranium mining and milling in the Southwest. The Sioux and Spokane Indian people in South Dakota and Washington have also recently been confronted by the booming industry. Uranium activity is now also affecting the native peoples of Saskatchewan and British Columbia in Canada.

Because of the spiritual significance of Mount Taylor, members of the Navajo Medicinemen's Association and the spiritual leaders of Acoma and Hopi pueblos spoke and offered blessings in support of the anti-uranium mining demands. Hopi elder David Monongye told of the Hopi prophecy about the coming of the "Danger Time" of ecological catastrophe if people don't respect the earth. The respected leader compared the mountain to a church of the non-Indians. "It must not be torn down or destroyed," he said.

"Those who want the mountain are like a crackerjack," he said. "Like it says on the crackerjack box, 'the more you eat the more you want.' They are greedy people who are trying to take all our land away from us. But we're not going to let go of it; this land is ours."

Medicineman James Watchempino of Acoma Pueblo told the gathering: "We all know the big oil companies want to try and destroy our beautiful mountains and our mother earth. The elders still remember when this country was beautiful. Now we don't breath fresh air and don't see so many birds anymore.". . .

A Worldwide Threat to Indian People

The Indian people of North America are not the only indigenous people to face the threat of nuclear power development. Australian-born physician, author and anti-nuclear activist Helen Caldicott told the Indians of New Mexico about her recent trip to Australia where the U.S. firms have discovered what may be the richest deposit of uranium in the world under aboriginal land.

"Their land is their religion, and, like you Indians, they worship the land," she said in an emotional speech. "What Gulf is doing

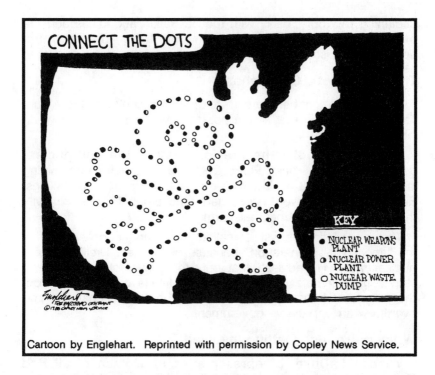

Cartoon by Englehart. Reprinted with permission by Copley News Service.

to your land, Gulf is doing in Australia to sacred aboriginal land. All the oil companies and multinationals are in Australia about to destroy aboriginal land.

"We, the white people, have nearly destroyed you — the people who got the answers to the mysteries of life and the mysteries of the universe. You mustn't let us destroy you anymore," she said.

"Right here at Mount Taylor starts the nuclear fuel cycle, and the young Indian men who will be mining it will be dying of lung cancer. They will die of dreadful pain and will cough up blood," asserted Caldicott, who said the slogan of the aborigines is "Land Rights, Not Mining."

At the National No Nuclear Strategy Conference last summer, John Redhouse, a AIEC director and organizer of the Mount Taylor rally stated "There is increasing opposition by Indian people to uranium exploration."

"Because Indians control so much of the country's uranium supply, they are in a position to potentially prevent much of the hazardous front end of the nuclear fuel cycle," he said.

The New Mexico Indian leader added that "Indian people are

beginning to work closely with the Australian aborigines and the black indigenous people of Namibia on the uranium developments issue."

The Apocalyptic Generation

George Wald, nobel laureate for physics, spoke at the Mount Taylor rally, saying that Indian people have been given the worst land to live on.

Wald, who spoke the previous day at the anti-nuclear demonstration at Rocky Flats, Colorado, said "Uranium mining isn't healthy; it isn't healthy to live near the mines or the tailings. Every dose is an overdose. There's no amount of radioactivity that is released that does not harm."

The white-haired physicist called the young people of today the "apocalyptic generation" because of the near likelihood of a nuclear war. He advised that only the power of people could stop a nuclear catastrophe. We should take our example from the people of Iran who went out into the streets unarmed and overthrew an oppressive government.

Women Are Also Getting Involved

Winona LaDuke, a representative of Women of all Red Nations, asked that women take a "special responsibility" to stop nuclear development and the exploitation of Indian land.

"When we take uranium out of the ground, it affects the women first through the fetuses and our children," she said. "Power is now in the hands of the men who created the technology, the few people who control our land and lives, our children and our resources."

The Indian leader quoted the Cherokee proverb: "A nation is not destroyed until the hearts of the women are on the ground."

She warned though that nuclear power is only one small part of the monster facing the people of the United States. "We are fighting the biggest companies in the world and the government endorses them and subsidizes them and helps them onto Indian land," said LaDuke.

WHAT IS EDITORIAL BIAS?

This activity may be used as an individualized study guide for students in libraries and resource centers or as a discussion catalyst in small group and classroom discussions.

The capacity to recognize an author's point of view is an essential reading skill. The skill to read with insight and understanding involves the ability to detect different kinds of opinions or bias. Sex bias, race bias, ethnocentric bias, political bias, and religious bias are five basic kinds of opinions expressed in editorials and all literature that attempts to persuade. They are briefly defined below.

Five Kinds of Editorial Opinion or Bias

SEX BIAS—The expression of dislike for and/or feeling of superiority over the opposite sex or a particular sexual minority.

RACE BIAS—The expression of dislike for and/or feeling of superiority over a racial group.

ETHNOCENTRIC BIAS—The expression of a belief that one's own group, race, religion, culture, or nation is superior. Ethnocentric persons judge others by their own standards and values.

POLITICAL BIAS—The expression of political opinions and attitudes about domestic or foreign affairs.

RELIGIOUS BIAS—The expression of a religious belief or attitude.

Guidelines

1. From the readings in Chapter Two, locate five sentences that provide examples of editorial opinion or bias.

2. Write down each of the above sentences and determine what kind of bias each sentence represents. Is it *sex bias, race bias, ethnocentric bias, political bias, or religious bias?*

3. Make up one sentence statements that would be an example of each of the following: *sex bias, race bias, ethnocentric bias, political bias, and religious bias.*

4. See if you can locate five sentences that are factual statements from the readings in Chapter Two.

CHAPTER 3

STORING NUCLEAR WASTE

8   STORING NUCLEAR WASTE

PROGRESS IN NUCLEAR WASTE STORAGE

Benard C. Rusche

Benard C. Rusche testified in his capacity as director of the Office of Civilian Radioactive Waste Management, Department of Energy.

Points to Consider:

1. What observations does the author offer regarding the nuclear waste program?

2. When does the Office of Civilian Radioactive Waste Management expect to have a geologic repository in operation? Why?

3. Describe the elements which the author believes will provide constructive adjustments in order to move ahead with the program.

Excerpted from the testimony of Benard C. Rusche before the House Subcommittee on Energy and Power to the House Committee on Energy and Commerce, October 16, 1987.

*The technical progress made thus far in the program
has been very encouraging in spite of the institutional
difficulties.*

I appreciate the opportunity to appear before you today to discuss nuclear waste legislation relating to the Civilian Radioactive Waste Management program. . . .

The national program has made considerable progress and has also reached the point where we can now identify where adjustments are needed to successfully continue toward the major goal established by the Nuclear Waste Policy Act of 1982 (NWPA).

A Few Observations

The Department of Energy (DOE) is pleased to see action in Congress that holds considerable promise for correcting some of the deficiencies in solving the complex problems of implementing the nuclear waste program. But before discussing some of the legislative proposals, I would like to briefly make a few observations.

First, spent nuclear fuel and high-level radioactive waste continue to accumulate and the need for disposal continues to grow. This was clearly recognized by Congress in its passage of the NWPA.

Second, our confidence in the basic principles and blueprint formulated by Congress in the NWPA continues unabated. We believe that permanent geologic disposal, deep underground, in a stable rock formation, coupled with integral Monitored Retrievable Storage (MRS) is the right course for this nation.

Third, the technical progress made thus far in the program has been very encouraging in spite of the institutional difficulties. Among the technical accomplishments we have made since passage of the NWPA are the approval by the President in 1986 of the Secretary of Energy's recommendation of three sites for detailed site characterization, submittal to Congress of the MRS proposal and the dedication of two new dry storage demonstration installations for more efficient at-reactor storage until DOE begins to receive spent fuel for disposal.

Congressional Direction

There have been long and numerous conversations about the progress, problems, and pace of implementing the NWPA and developing the waste disposal system and about our ability to

MONITORED RETRIEVAL STORAGE

The nation requires that a technically sound and publically acceptable high-level radioactive waste disposal program be developed for the commercial use of nuclear energy to be able to continue. Thus, it is the industry's overriding goal to achieve efficient, effective, and fair implementation of the Nuclear Waste Policy Act (NWPA) leading to the successful operation of a national high-level radioactive waste disposal system as close to the NWPA's schedule as possible. A monitored retrieval storage facility will perform functions essential to the timely disposal of spent fuel. It will provide vitally needed flexibility in the planning, design, construction, and operation of the disposal system. Inclusion of a MRS will enable progress to be made towards the operation of the national disposal system earlier than would be the case with a repository-only system. It would provide a location for preparing spent fuel for disposal as well as serving as a transportation hub for the movement of spent fuel from reactors to the repository. The MRS would consolidate fuel (if required), package it for disposal, and also provide a limited amount of storage.

Excerpted from the testimony of Northeast Utilities before the House Subcommittee on Energy and Power of the House Committee on Energy and Commerce, June 11, 1987

work effectively with affected and interested parties. Our commitment remains to work diligently to carry out the will of Congress in a technically sound and publicly open manner with affected and interested parties. We are pleased that Congress is actively addressing solutions in the constructive way evidenced by the recommendations of many members of Congress.

In the Mission Plan Amendment submitted by the Office of Civilian Radioactive Waste Management to Congress in June, some modifications to the Department's waste program were presented. And through that vehicle, we requested Congressional direction. We requested Congressional action to implement our best judgment that the siting of a second repository be postponed until well into the next century. We noted that the earliest we could predict operation of a geologic repository was advanced to 2003 to allow time to meet technical and institutional objectives. We reiterated our findings presented in the MRS proposal to Congress that an MRS should be an integral part of the waste disposal system and requested approval to proceed. And we suggested that Congress consider providing substantial financial or other incentives for a state or an Indian Tribe to work cooperatively with DOE.

Within the bills proposed in Congress are a variety of changes ranging from starting over to providing additional financial incentives for states to work with DOE and to host a repository or an MRS.

Constructive Elements in the Legislation

We have provided specific answers to questions you asked on various pieces of legislation. In this brief statement, I believe we may establish a better framework for discussions by listing constructive elements in the legislation rather than reiterating details from the questions and answers. Essentially, we believe the following elements of pending legislation may provide constructive adjustments that would enable us to move ahead with the program in a sound technical way without sacrificing progress that has been made.

● Sequential characterization of sites for repository;

● Authorization for an MRS as an integral part of the waste management system; and

● Suspension of site-specific work on a second repository and reviewing the need for a second repository approximately 20 years from now.

We believe that financial incentive payments would be appropriate for a potential host. Additionally, the concept of a volunteer for technical consideration for an MRS or a repository may also be worthy of consideration. In addition, as I have previously stated, and as stated in the Mission Plan Amendment, we urge Congressional action that would provide for direct participation by local governments as well as additional flexibility in the definition of the units of local government to which the DOE would be allowed to make payments under the NWPA's provisions for payments equal to taxes. (DOE is currently restrained from making such payments to special units of local government.)

More Constructive Elements

Two other elements that we believe may have merit are consideration of a special negotiator to work with states, Indian Tribes, and DOE in developing consultation and cooperation and

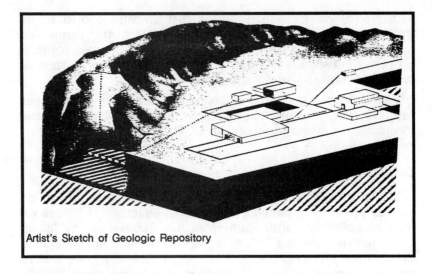
Artist's Sketch of Geologic Repository

also expanded involvement by the National Academy of Sciences.

These are but basic concepts proposed in pending legislation which we believe could be all or in part constructive modifications to the already existing important national mandate and roadmap represented by the NWPA. Details of the design and implementation of any or all of these concepts, in our opinion, would require careful, but sensitive, crafting and attention.

THE WASTE PROGRAM IS IN RUINS

Richard H. Bryan

Richard H. Bryan testified before the Subcommittee on Energy and the Environment in his capacity as governor of Nevada.

Points to Consider:

1. Why are the citizens of Nevada demanding to be treated fairly?

2. According to the author, what is the matter with the Senate Energy Committee's proposal?

3. What are the two types of state concerns?

Excerpted from the testimony of Richard H. Bryan before the House Subcommittee on Energy and the Environment of the House Committee on Interior and Insular Affairs, September 18, 1987.

As Chairman Udall so aptly and succinctly stated: "the [nuclear waste repository] program is in ruins."

Despite the rhetoric and political charades and denials that are coming from some Congressional quarters, all the major players in fact seem to have come to understand and accept that Nevada and other states, tribes, and environmental groups have been quite correct in saying that the current Department of Energy (DOE) repository program is fatally flawed. . . .

Thus, the real issue here is how Congress should deal with this problem, not whether the problem exists. The time has come for a very forthright and candid discussion of this critical question. . . .

Time for a Fresh Start

Nevadans are outraged that some in Congress, who appear intent on disregarding basic fairness and the factual record, are seeking in effect to ram the repository down our throats because they mistakenly believe that it is politically expedient to do so. The recent Senate Energy Committee legislation, which has just been attached to the energy and water appropriations bill, adopts this irresponsible approach and attempts to circumvent normal procedures and Congress' intent in the 1982 Act.

Let no one misread the signals coming from our state or misunderstand our position: the vast majority of Nevadans are united in strongly opposing any such unprincipled and misdirected legislative proposals. We will fight as we have never fought before to prevent a repository from being forced upon us. While we remain committed to working constructively and in good faith with any interested party to develop workable legislative solutions, we demand to be treated fairly.

Instead of pursuing the short-sighted and politically motivated legislative approach taken by the Senate Energy Committee, Congress should rather be working constructively toward "fine tuning" the 1982 Act, which contains a sound basic framework for siting high-level waste facilities. This can be done by crafting amendments after receiving the recommendations of an independent review commission. At the same time, it appears reasonable to attempt to seek out a state willing to host a repository in exchange for reasonable assurances of safety and other benefits.

Although the siting process can be repaired, this will require a "fresh start" because the original site selections were made improperly, and the current DOE program is so totally lacking in public credibility and acceptability. Many major program actions, including the candidate site selections, were made in violation of the Act's requirements and must be rolled back and re-implemented to correct fatal flaws. Fortunately, as I will discuss, there is still ample time to restore public acceptability and confidence that the site-selection process will produce a safe repository by developing appropriate necessary "mid-course corrections," and making a "fresh start" to place the program firmly back on its intended track.

The Senate Energy Committee's Defective Legislation

Because this Committee may have to deal with the Senate Energy Committee proposal, I will briefly highlight our objections to that measure. . . .

In effect, the Energy Committee is proposing to scrap the 1982 Act's concept of selecting a safe site by fair, objective, and credible procedures. This legislation requires the Secretary of Energy to choose one of the three sites selected for characterization and to characterize and seek to license only that site. The state that hosts a chosen site could receive substantial financial payments for as long as the site is a viable candidate or operational repository, but only if the state does not seek to veto or otherwise contest DOE's decisions regarding the site's suitability. (Moreover, the bill does not permit a state not currently designated as a candidate site to volunteer to host the facility and be eligible for additional payments.) In addition to trying to buy support from the host state, the Senate Energy

Committee bill tries to buy political support from other states by postponing until well into the next century the second-round siting process and by vacating the present Monitored Retrievable Storage (MRS) site selection and requiring additional siting activities for the MRS. This Senate proposal also limits judicial review of the DOE's actions, restricts the application of environmental safeguards, and incorporates additional siting priorities, such as a cost emphasis, intentionally designed to bias the site-selection process toward choosing the Nevada site. This bill even appears to nullify our pending litigation under the 1982 Act. For example, it could be argued that after our site was selected as the preferred site, a court could then rule in one of our pending lawsuits that Nevada should not have been selected for characterization under the 1982 Act, yet we nevertheless could be forced to be characterized under the new title, with no right of appeal.

The Senate Committee's bill, when stripped of its shamefully transparent window dressing, is little more than a blatant attempt to ram the repository down the throat of an unwilling state, which most informed parties conclude would be Nevada under the Committee's new priority criteria. It is patently clear that the nominations of Nevada, Washington, and Texas for site characterization were improper and unjustified because they were based on an illegal and unfair siting process that violated the 1982 Act's requirements. Nevertheless, the Johnston-McClure legislation would change the law and treat these invalid selections as though they were legitimate and justified! It then proceeds to focus the future siting efforts on us.

This Senate Energy approach is grossly unfair and lacks technical credibility. Nevadans will never accept having a repository forced upon them under such circumstances. We are astounded that Congress would even seriously consider such an unprincipled and irresponsible approach. Let there be no misunderstanding: Nevada is not a nuclear wasteland, nor is it a panacea for DOE's misdirected repository program. Yucca Mountain has not been demonstrated to be uniquely qualified to best serve the national purpose of providing safe and acceptable nuclear waste disposal. Many well substantiated and serious scientific questions have been raised by both Nevada and the Nuclear Regulatory Commission as to whether Yucca Mountain could ever be licensed under existing rules and criteria. Moreover, our citizens are overwhelmingly opposed to having the repository. Public confidence in this program has been destroyed by DOE's improper and irresponsible actions, and it

DEPARTMENT OF ENERGY URANIUM WASTE DUMP

Illustration by Paul Conrad. © 1988, The Times. Reprinted by permission of Los Angeles Times Syndicate.

cannot be restored through coercion and bribery. We will fight this unjustifiable Senate Energy Committee legislation with all of our resources, and I will assure those who are supporting that approach that it ultimately will not work. Moreover, it will prove to be far more costly and time consuming than they ever imagined and add enormously to the utility ratepayers' burdens. . . .

Two Distinct Types of State Concerns

It is quite important to recognize that Nevada and the other states have raised two separate types of basic concerns, neither of which can be disregarded:

- *Scientific and Technical Concerns.* We have expressed concerns of a scientific and technical nature that have involved both: (a) whether our sites are safe and licensable under existing law and regulations (many of which appear to be legally defective); and (b) serious objections to DOE's failure to seek and fully consider potentially disqualifying data, the validity of certain data that have been collected, and the questionable methodologies and overly optimistic interpretations that DOE has given to much of this data.

- *Legal and Process Concerns.* We also have objected strongly to DOE's repeated failure to comply with the Act's requirements. Our objections are not grounded in mere politics or "not-in-my-backyard" attitudes. Instead, our concerns are quite legitimate and have arisen because DOE has failed to comply with the provisions and intent of the law. Politics have played a role, however, in DOE's decision making, and some of DOE's departures from the Act have occurred because of blatantly political considerations. (A clear example of this can be seen in DOE's attempt to indefinitely postpone the Second-Round siting process by administrative action, despite the Act's express provisions and obvious intent.) In other instances, DOE has taken improper actions for reasons that need not be termed "political," at least in the partisan sense. Such actions appear to be motivated by DOE program officials' predispositions and what might be called bureaucratic, "mission-driven" thinking.

The states, in accord with the findings of the 1982 Act, always have deemed the second category of objections concerning DOE's serious violations of the Act's requirements to be as fundamental as the technical and scientific objections in the first category. Thus, we can never simply "forgive and forget" DOE's past biased, improper and illegal actions. Nevada, Texas, and Washington clearly were selected for site characterization through a very biased and political process that did not follow the Act's requirements. Acceptance of these tainted selections therefore is simply out of the question. Any viable legislative solution must roll-back these flawed and invalid decisions and provide for a "fresh start" when evaluating our sites.

NUCLEAR WASTE IS NO SERIOUS THREAT

Alvin M. Weinberg

Alvin M. Weinberg has been associated with the nuclear energy enterprise since its beginning. He served as director of the Oak Ridge National Laboratory from 1955 to 1974; he served as director of the Office of Energy Research and Development in 1974; and he directed the Institute for Energy Analysis from 1975 to 1985.

Points to Consider:

1. Why has the radioactive waste issue evoked such bitter opposition on the part of the public?

2. What barriers would block the path of radioactive waste to the biosphere?

3. Describe Sweden's chemically safe waste disposal package. How does it work?

4. Do you agree that compensation should be offered to a state that accepts a repository? Why or why not?

Excerpted from the testimony of Alvin M. Weinberg before the Senate Committee on Energy and Natural Resources, April 28, 1987.

I applaud attempts to educate the public as to the insignificance of radiation exposure at the level estimated to come from a repository.

I have been involved in the problem of waste disposal, mainly as a laboratory administrator, since the early 1950s. However, I do not regard myself as a specialist in waste disposal; my technical knowledge of the field derives from long association with people at Oak Ridge National Laboratory who were responsible for laboratory programs in waste disposal.

As early as 1952, Professor James Conant, President of Harvard and President Roosevelt's wartime advisor on atomic energy, predicted that the world would turn away from nuclear energy because the problem of waste disposal would prove to be difficult to manage. A good part of my energy, as director of the Oak Ridge National Laboratory, was directed toward proving that Professor Conant was wrong.

Not a Difficult Technical Problem

And indeed, if one were to judge by the estimates of most technical people, radioactive waste disposal is, almost without exception, not regarded as being a particularly difficult technical problem. It does not, for example, compare in difficulty with the problem of reactor safety. In the latter case, nuclear experts had realized from the outset that a reactor, generating enormous amounts of heat (which cannot be turned off) could be a serious hazard. In the case of the wastes, the heat generated is far smaller; there is no powerful driving force, which, if uncontained, could cause a massive spread of radioactivity.

Why then has the radioactive waste issue evoked such bitter opposition on the part of the public? Until Three Mile Island and Chernobyl, it evoked much greater public concern than had the issue of reactor accident. I believe one important reason is the widespread misunderstanding as to the hazards of low levels of radiation. There is essentially no credible scenario connected with the entire waste disposal cycle—temporary storage above ground, transport, final disposal in a geologic depository—which imposes on any individual a really large dose of radiation. This contrasts sharply with reactor accidents; at Chernobyl, for example, many people received lethal doses of radiation. I believe the public, in expressing its fear of nuclear wastes, tends to compound possible releases from a waste depository with the far more lethal releases from an uncontained reactor accident. Until and unless the public understands that doses of the order of background inconsequential, waste disposal, even nuclear energy itself, will founder. I therefore applaud attempts to educate the public as to the insignificance of radiation exposure at the level estimated to come from a repository.

In all fairness, there have been a few very improbable scenarios involving flooding of a repository which conceivably might lead to exposures, after many thousands of years, considerably higher than background. The most notable such estimate comes from a National Academy Report in which such exposures could not be absolutely ruled out, though the likelihood is minuscule, and the time for them to occur, extremely long.

Geologic Barriers

Are there approaches to waste disposal that would lay to rest even such residual concerns? I remind you that the safety of waste disposal is based on several barriers blocking the path from radioactive waste to the biosphere. These barriers are (1) the waste form itself—sintered UO_2 in the case of unreprocessed fuel, borosilicate glass for reprocessed wastes; (2) the container; (3) the overpack and backfill; (4) the geologic environment. A radioactive atom must traverse each of these barriers if it is to reach the biosphere.

The U.S. waste program has, from the beginning, emphasized the geologic emplacement as perhaps the primary barrier to incursion of the wastes on the biosphere. This is not to say that waste form or canister have been ignored. But I have the impression that the geologic barrier—salt, tuff, basalt—has been the main focus of the effort.

I have no quarrel with the emphasis placed on the geologic barrier. However, to *prove* that the geologic barrier will work as planned, and as calculated in the various waste scenarios, is not easy: geology and hydrology are less easy to understand than are chemistry and physics.

I would therefore suggest that the Office of Civilian Radioactive Waste Management ought to devote even more effort to developing what I would call "inherently safe waste disposal schemes"—that is schemes whose safety depends less centrally on the difficult to understand, and often controversial, geology and hydrology and more upon the easier to understand and less controversial, chemistry and physics. What this amounts to is developing waste packages (waste forms, canisters, and overpacks) that are completely resistant even if the depository is invaded by water, for much longer than the 300-1,000 years required by the Nuclear Regulation Commission (NRC).

Safe Waste Disposal

I am not able to say exactly how long is long enough—especially since the *existing* systems, designed for 300 to 1,000 years, are already safe enough. But these systems depend for their ultimate safety on geology and hydrology. I suggest that systems that depend for safety less on geology and more on chemistry ought to be less subject to dispute by nuclear skeptics.

Sweden has developed such an approach; it plans to encase spent fuel in stout copper canisters. These are to be placed in geologic strata where native copper is found: the existence of native copper is prima facie evidence that the groundwater in the repository would not attack the waste canister. The Swedish public seems to have bought this scheme as satisfying a legislative requirement for "certainly safe" waste disposal.

Several technical paths toward achieving a "chemically" safe—i.e., an inherently safe waste package might be considered. For example, the sintered UO_2 itself apparently completely binds plutonium and other transuranics; thus the National Academy study may have been much more pessimistic than was justified in this respect. Again, several suggestions for sintered aluminum oxide—i.e., sapphire—cans have been put forward on the ground that sapphire is totally resistant to groundwater in many environments. But I do not want to guess what a chemically safe package might be; I do insist that

74

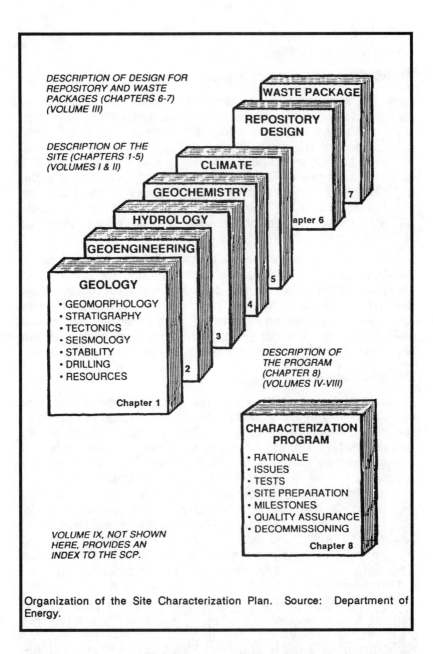

Organization of the Site Characterization Plan. Source: Department of Energy.

Sweden has come up with a chemically safe package, and the Swedish public seem to agree with the judgment that copper cans are chemically safe. I urge the Office of Civilian Radioactive Waste Management (OCRWM) to pay more attention to the development of a chemically safe package – one that would last, for example, 10,000 or more years even in a flooded hydrologic environment.

An Additional Margin of Safety

In this connection I was pleased to learn that OCRWM, in response to a directive of the Senate, has conducted a two-year study of the use of copper containers in basalt and in tuff. The conclusions of the study have been favorable. The general thrust of my recommendation is simply that I believe OCRWM ought to strengthen efforts such as this and, assuming that the experimental results are favorable, to convey to the public an understanding that the inherent or chemical safety of the waste package confers an additional margin of safety on a system that is already extremely safe.

Should this approach be successful, then it probably means that the waste will have to cool above ground for about 50 to 100 years, rather than for the originally designed 10 years. At the end of 100 years, the heat produced per minute by a spent fuel element is only one-fourth the heat produced per minute after 10 years. This simplifies repository design, and all but eliminates a variable—temperature—from consideration.

Compensation

I do not know whether incorporating the requirement of chemical safety in the repository design will change the minds of the many people who hate all things nuclear and especially nuclear wastes. I propose the approach *not* because I believe it is *necessary* to assure a technical person like myself that the repository is safe; it is rather that, in lessening dependence on difficult to define geologic and hydrologic processes, and increasing dependence on chemistry, we can make an easier case for convincing the public of the safety of the depository. Anyone can understand that if the can never leaks, no one can be harmed. It takes more sophistication to realize that some geologic barriers are also all but impossible to fail catastrophically.

The issue then is one of public perception. I have already alluded to the importance of the public's understanding the *in*significance of low levels of radiation. But even this may not be enough. I am therefore very pleased to learn that the proposed modification of the Nuclear Waste Policy Act proposes *generous* compensation for a state willing to accept a repository.

I believe the compensation should be awarded to a state in

which the depository is located regardless of the state's attitude. That is, I do not believe it wise to require public enthusiasm for a repository on the part of state politicians as a qualification for compensation. We must not put politicians in untenable, hardened positions. Even with compensation and chemically safe wastes, I doubt that the repository or the Monitored Retrievable Storage (MRS) will be welcomed, at least at the outset. I think it is asking too much of a politician to actually ask for a repository. On the other hand, with compensation I should think politicians could maintain a kind of neutrality, even benevolent neutrality, without jeopardizing their own political futures.

Conclusion

In conclusion, I should make clear that, from a purely technical viewpoint, the presently proposed system, with its strong reliance on geologic safety, is adequately safe. Nevertheless I favor continued and increased emphasis on development of inherently, chemically safe waste packages as a means of further reassuring a skeptical public. Finally, I strongly applaud the principle of compensation to the state and locale that is host to the repository, though I believe it unwise to make such compensation contingent on the enthusiasm with which the host state accepts the repository.

11   STORING NUCLEAR WASTE

THE GLOBAL THREAT OF NUCLEAR WASTE

International Physicians for the Prevention of Nuclear War

International Physicians for the Prevention of Nuclear War (IPPNW) was founded in 1980 to develop an international response to the medical dangers of nuclear war. IPPNW was awarded the Nobel Peace Prize in 1985 due, in part, "to the fact that the organization was formed as a result of a joint initiative by Soviet and American physicians and that it now draws support from physicians in over 40 countries all over the world."

Points to Consider:

1. Define the term "sacrifice zones."

2. Who is the PSR? How do they describe the nuclear waste problem?

3. What will IPPNW's International Commission attempt to do?

4. Describe the two factors IPPNW credits for its success.

Excerpted from a March 1989 public letter written by the International Physicians for the Prevention of Nuclear War, Inc.

If nuclear weapons production continues unabated and spreads to other countries, it offers a future prospect as ominous as the threat of nuclear annihilation itself.

It's bad enough that we have had to live all these years with the threat of nuclear annihilation.

What's worse is to discover that we've also had to pay a hidden price to sustain this nuclear madness.

I'm referring to the serious health and environmental consequences of nuclear weapons production recently revealed by U.S. government officials.

Only the Tip of the Iceberg

In line with IPPNW's mission to share the medical facts of nuclear war, here is what we know so far:

The radiation leakage in nuclear facilities has caused cancer in an unknown number of plant workers who live nearby. It will be years before we know the true extent of damage to the public health.

In some cases this leakage continues unabated.

Hazardous waste pollution from these plants has leached into the groundwater and is spreading every minute. There is no way to calculate the eventual toll this will have on the environment and all living things. . . plants, animals, and human beings.

There is serious talk in government circles of designating the communities around certain facilities as "sacrifice zones," because they are already beyond reclamation.

Nothing has been said about the men, women, and children who have been working and living in these zones.

We have only seen the tip of the iceberg.

A Threat to the Future

Most of the gross mismanagement of sensitive materials, the violation of elemental safety precautions, the irresponsible dumping of volatile waste. . .most of it has been hidden behind the cloak of military secrecy.

And what we have barely glimpsed in the United States has been completely hidden away in other nations. . .the Soviet

Union, France, Great Britain, China, India, Israel, South Africa, and Pakistan.

All are nuclear-capable and have on-going production programs—whether they admit it or not.

Nuclear weapons production, as it is conducted throughout the world, is a huge, but largely unknown, threat to the future of humankind.

Our United States affiliate, Physicians for Social Responsibility (PSR), calls the situation "a creeping Chernobyl." PSR is leading the way in the United States to bring the truth about nuclear weapons production to the public.

If nuclear weapons production continues unabated and spreads to other countries, it offers a future prospect as ominous as the threat of nuclear annihilation itself.

An International Commission

Immediate steps must be taken to determine the actual extent of this threat, to share that knowledge and to mobilize people to confront it.

After devoting nine years to educating people about the threat of nuclear war, International Physicians for the Prevention of Nuclear War (IPPNW), will expand its mission.

We intend to expose this "creeping Chernobyl" and organize world leadership and opinion to halt it.

IPPNW has established an International Commission to assess the public health hazards posed by nuclear weapons production.

Working with our physician affiliates in each country, the Commission will attempt

- to identify all nuclear production facilities, their worker populations, and threats to surrounding communities;
- to seek data on releases of radioactivity and toxic chemicals at these facilities; and
- to project the impact nuclear weapons production is having on public health and the environment.

Together with our Soviet colleagues we have called upon Mikhail Gorbachev and George Bush to take the lead in lifting the veil of secrecy surrounding the public health consequences of nuclear weapons production in their countries.

IPPNW's campaign is consistent with our mission. We were founded in 1980 to develop an international response to the medical dangers of nuclear war.

And our success so far has been based on two facts. One is that physicians can play a significant part in the movement to halt the nuclear arms race. The other is that an organization against nuclear war which involves both Soviets and Americans exercises unusual influence.

Nobel Peace Prize

In awarding IPPNW the 1985 Nobel Peace Prize, the Norwegian Nobel Committee attached "particular importance to the fact that the organization was formed as a result of a joint initiative by Soviet and American physicians and that it now draws support from physicians in over 40 countries all over the world."

IPPNW's Global Campaign

IPPNW now has affiliates in 61 countries. And that number continues to grow.

These unique human resources enable us to carry on international campaigns that reach around the globe.

Along with our new International Commission on Nuclear Weapons Production, we will also continue our efforts to halt nuclear test explosions throughout the Cease Fire '89 campaign.

From Argentina to Zambia, from the United States to the

Illustration by David Seavey. Copyright 1989, *USA Today*. Reprinted with permission.

Soviet Union, IPPNW doctors are responding to every nuclear test explosion. Leaders in testing countries are being challenged to face up to the health and medical consequences of their actions.

ABOVE GROUND STORAGE: POINTS AND COUNTERPOINTS

William W. Berry vs. Tennessee Nuclear Waste Task Force

William W. Berry, chairman of Virginia Power, testified on behalf of Edison Electric Institute, American Nuclear Energy Council, Utility Nuclear Waste Management Group, Electric Utility Companies' Nuclear Transportation Group, and Atomic Industrial Forum.

The Tennessee Nuclear Waste Task Force is composed of citizen groups, business associations, churches, and other people concerned about Department of Energy waste programs.

Points to Consider:

1. Why does Mr. Berry claim that the General Accounting Office's fact sheet was misleading?

2. According to Mr. Berry, what are some of the MRS advantages?

3. Does there have to be an MRS? Please explain your answer.

4. What kind of false information did University of Tennessee researchers seek to correct?

Excerpted from the testimony of William W. Berry before the Senate Committee on Energy and Natural Resources, April 29, 1987, and from the testimony of the Tennessee Nuclear Waste Task Force before the House Subcommittee on Energy and Power of the House Committee on Energy and Commerce, June 11, 1987.

THE POINT—by William W. Berry

The nation requires development of a technically sound and publicly acceptable high-level radioactive waste disposal program for commercial use of nuclear energy to continue. In this regard, it is the industry's overriding goal to achieve efficient, effective, and fair implementation of the Nuclear Waste Policy Act of 1982 (NWPA) leading to the successful operation of a national high-level radioactive waste disposal system as close to the NWPA schedule as possible. By authorizing, funding, and not restricting the use of the Monitored Retrievable Storage (MRS) facility, Congress would be taking a large step towards this end.

Industry Support

The industry supports — unequivocally — the need for the MRS. Through its CEO committees and association boards of directors, the industry adopted a policy in support of the MRS. . . . It is unfortunate that opponents of the MRS try to exploit the different opinions held by a few individuals within the industry in an attempt to show that industry support for the MRS is lacking. The General Accounting Office (GAO), in its May 1986 Fact Sheet, reported misleading survey results that seemed to show a lack of full industry support for the MRS. These misleading results were the product of a survey questionnaire that simply asked the wrong questions.

MRS Advantages

As an integral part of the high-level radioactive waste disposal system, the MRS will perform functions essential to the disposal of spent fuel. It will provide vitally needed flexibility in the planning, design, construction, and operation of the disposal system, thereby lessening the effects of the uncertainties that DOE faces. Furthermore, the NWPA implementation experience thus far has demonstrated that progress is, indeed, a precious commodity. The MRS is an important item that will make progress towards the operation of the disposal system earlier than would be the case with a repository-only system. Having the MRS in the disposal system would help bring the first repository into operation sooner by allowing a more flexible and efficient repository design and licensing process. The nuclear industry supports the development of an MRS as an integral part of the repository program. However, the MRS is not acceptable for long-term disposal, which must be accomplished in a deep underground repository. DOE has raised the importance of the

Illustration by Web Bryant. Copyright 1987, *USA Today.* Reprinted with permission

MRS by planning to use the facility to live up to its statutory and contractual obligation to accept spent fuel by January 31, 1998. If Congress accepts this NWPA implementation change, then Congress must authorize, fund, and not restrict the use of the MRS. The MRS would be a vital part of the nation's high-level radioactive waste disposal system. It would provide a location for preparing spent fuel for disposal as well as serve as a transportation hub for the movement of spent fuel from reactors to the repository. The MRS would consolidate fuel (if required) and package it for disposal, which are functions that must, in any event, be part of the above ground element of a repository system. It would also provide a limited amount of storage. These are important functions necessary for the disposal of spent fuel; however, there are stronger reasons for including an MRS as part of the high-level radioactive waste disposal system: flexibility and progress. . . .

Foreign Disposal Programs

There has been much recent discussion of the high-level radioactive waste disposal programs in several European countries. It is important to recognize that every one of these programs, especially in France, West Germany and Sweden, has the disposal of high-level radioactive waste in deep geologic repositories as its ultimate goal. Their schedules differ from ours and the specific activities they will pursue are somewhat different, because of their different regulatory and institutional structures. Nonetheless, the ultimate goal—disposal in deep geologic repositories—is the same.

Most countries appear to be making progress towards ultimate disposal by the use of a central collection, preparation, and interim storage facility. France, West Germany, and Sweden plan to dispose eventually of their nuclear waste in deep underground geologic repositories. However, each has planned central interim facilities for spent fuel or high-level waste prior to ultimate disposal. In France, spent fuel is placed in water pools at the reprocessing plant site, subsequently reprocessed, and the separated high-level waste solidified by classification into waste packages for disposal at a later date. The same general approach is planned for West Germany except the spent fuel is placed in dry storage casks at a central facility prior to reprocessing. In Sweden, the quantity of spent fuel is limited to their specific nuclear program and it is being placed in a central water pool facility for an extended period before being packaged for placement in a geologic repository without reprocessing. The U.S. can also begin to make progress towards disposal if Congress authorizes, funds, and does not restrict the use of the MRS facility.

THE COUNTERPOINT—Tennessee Nuclear Waste Task Force

What Is an MRS?

The Department of Energy (DOE) has proposed constructing a Monitored Retrievable Storage (MRS) facility at the abandoned Clinch River Breeder site near Oak Ridge, Tennessee. Utilities with nuclear reactors east of the Rockies would ship their irradiated fuel to Oak Ridge. There, DOE would take the irradiated fuel assemblies apart and pack the fuel rods closer (consolidation). This repackaging would occur above ground using robotics in a hot cell. The consolidated irradiated fuel would then be placed into large concrete storage casks for above ground storage until a geologic repository was readied for permanent disposal of the fuel. If and when a repository is established, the irradiated fuel would be placed into transportation casks and shipped on a train that would carry only nuclear wastes (dedicated train) to the repository.

Why Does the DOE Want the MRS?

The DOE claims many benefits for an MRS such as early acceptance of irradiated fuel from utilities, decreasing the need for additional storage at reactors, simplification of repository operations, an improved transportation system, and development of institutional experiences that can be applied to repository siting.

All of these benefits are also shared by an optimized

at-reactor storage option. The question arises: Why DOE has put so much effort behind justifying an unnecessary MRS while at the same time discrediting any at-reactor option.

There are two basic reasons why DOE has chosen this path. First, the Nuclear Waste Policy Act (NWPA) sets 1998 as the date for acceptance of irradiated fuel from utilities for disposal at a repository. An MRS that was operating in 1998 would create the image that DOE had met the NWPA deadline. Secondly, an operating or even authorized MRS would create the national image that progress was being made in the decades long search for nuclear waste management. The MRS would create the illusion that the nuclear waste problem is being solved.

Does There Have to Be an MRS?

DOE in both its Mission Plan and MRS proposal clearly states that an MRS is not necessary for the successful operation of a nuclear waste disposal program. It has tried to create the sense of crisis that unless the MRS is immediately built, nuclear utilities will be forced to shut down and the entire nuclear waste program thrown into disarray. DOE, however, has failed to compare its MRS option with other optimized nuclear waste management systems that even improve upon the MRS option.

Before the decision is made to pursue a central repackaging and storage facility, the option of an optimized no-MRS waste system should be fairly examined in depth. At-reactor waste preparation and storage would replace the need for a centralized repackaging and storage facility. Cask design, preparation of spent fuel for repository disposal, and transportation system controls are key elements to this system, making it safer and less costly. . . .

Tennessee Corrects DOE False Information on MRS

The State of Tennessee has over the past two years been doing the work DOE chose to ignore. University of Tennessee researchers funded through the state have reached results that DOE has been forced to acknowledge as correct, although these findings are not reflected in any of DOE's MRS promotional material.

- DOE said that the MRS would reduce waste transport miles. Tennessee researchers found that if transportation system improvements were made in a no-MRS option, there would be no transportation benefits with an MRS.

- DOE claims nearly $1 billion in utility benefits due to decreased need for utilities to build additional storage pools if the MRS is built. Tennessee researchers found that DOE overestimated irradiated fuel discharge rates in the year 2020 by 50 percent and that DOE failed to consider emerging reactor practices that would decrease additional storage needs. The utility benefit is thus closer to $100 million.

- Analysis by the State of Tennessee estimates that the net cost of adding an MRS to the nuclear waste system would range from $2.2 to 2.8 billion, about $1 billion more than estimated by DOE. The agency overestimated some of the benefits and failed to account for other costs. There is at best a 1:4 benefit cost ratio. This figure does not include any possible compensation (bribe package) Congress may confer upon nuclear waste facility host states.

How Permanent Is Temporary?

A concern that Tennessee has is that the MRS will become the de facto waste repository, as DOE's and the nation's attention will become focused on getting the MRS operational and shipping the nuclear waste to it. Once the irradiated fuel is dumped off onto the backroads of Tennessee, the national pressure will be off DOE to find a safe and technically sound method to permanently dispose of the irradiated fuel and high level wastes.

To avoid this possibility, DOE has proposed linking the operation of the MRS to the Nuclear Regulatory Commission, permitting the construction of a geologic repository and then limiting the storage of irradiated fuel at the MRS to 3,000 metric tons until the repository is operational.

There are two problems with this "coupling" of the MRS to the repository. The first is that both DOE and Congress could at anytime choose to undo this linkage.

Secondly, if operation of the MRS were truly tied to the construction of the repository, any further delay in repository siting would obviate any of the benefits the MRS would have to the integrated nuclear waste management system. Potentially, the DOE could scrap the repository program and the MRS would be our nation's answer to its nuclear waste problems.

Tennessee Says "Not in Anybody's Backyard!"

Tennessee is doing more research in such areas as waste preparation technologies and determination of the true costs of the MRS, all work that DOE has failed to do because of its own subjective determination that it would rather have MRS.

DOE's remaining claimed benefits for the MRS are highly conjectural and subjective. They are not sufficient to justify the potential hazards and costs of the MRS to the ratepayers, to Tennessee, and to communities along the shipment routes. Congress needs to understand that the MRS is unneeded. While Tennessee may be saying it does not want an MRS in Tennessee, it is also saying that it does not have to be anywhere. Congress must be given the opportunity to decide.

STORING NUCLEAR WASTE

TRANSPORTING NUCLEAR WASTE: POINTS AND COUNTERPOINTS

Charles E. Kay vs. William L. Clay

Charles E. Kay testified in his capacity as acting director of the Office of Civilian Radioactive Waste Management, U.S. Department of Energy (DOE).

William L. Clay testified in his capacity as a U.S. Representative from the State of Missouri.

Points to Consider:

1. How will DOE program reorganization help improve transportation considerations?

2. Describe DOE's safety record with regard to nuclear waste transportation.

3. According to Representative Clay's observations, what factors does DOE consider in selecting a transportation route?

4. Why does Representative Clay describe the federal laws pertinent to the shipment of radioactive materials as "convoluted, fragmented, and wrought with ambiguity?"

Excerpted from the testimony of Charles E. Kay and William L. Clay before the House Subcommittee on Energy and Environment of the House Committee on Interior and Insular Affairs, May 12, 1988.

THE POINT — by Charles E. Kay

In developing transportation capabilities as an essential element of the waste-management system, we are fortunate to be able to build on a long history of safe shipping experience and a comprehensive system of federal regulation and international standards. Because the schedule for the transportation program is linked to the schedule for the development and operation of waste disposal and storage facilities—with operation of a repository expected to begin in the year 2003 and a monitored retrievable storage (MRS) facility between 1998 and 2003—we are also afforded unique opportunities and adequate time to refine and improve shipping equipment and procedures, and to coordinate transportation planning with other federal agencies, industry, states, Indian tribes, and all other interested parties. I believe that we have made real progress in terms of technical developments and in addressing institutional concerns—some of which form the basis of legislative proposals now being considered by the Congress. . . .

Program Reorganization

Significantly, under the new organization structure, we continue to recognize transportation as a key component of the waste-management system and the importance of coordinating transportation planning with other elements of the waste-management program. With the organization now restructured along functional lines instead of project lines, we can better incorporate transportation considerations into the design and operation of all the other components of the system.

Continued emphasis will also remain on the well-established objectives of the transportation program: to ensure that activities are performed in a safe, secure, and efficient manner, using private industry to the greatest extent possible; to comply with all applicable laws and regulations; and to foster broad-based public understanding of, and participation in, program planning. As a specific indication of the growing importance we are placing on transportation, our Fiscal Year 1988 budget for transportation activities shows a 50 percent increase over Fiscal Year 1987, and our request for Fiscal Year 1989 is 33 percent greater than our Fiscal Year 1988 budget. . . .

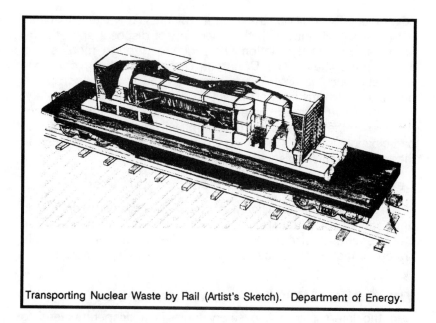
Transporting Nuclear Waste by Rail (Artist's Sketch). Department of Energy.

Shipping Experience

When developing plans and procedures for the Nuclear Waste Policy Act of 1982 (NWPA) shipping, the Department of Energy (DOE) will rely on the considerable commercial and noncommercial shipping experience gained over the past 40 years. Existing DOE transportation programs—primarily in the DOE's Office of Defense Programs—for shipping noncommercial nuclear materials provide a source of expertise for operations, policy, and procedures.

It is important to note that shipping conducted to date by both DOE and utilities under existing regulations has demonstrated the safety of spent fuel and high-level radioactive waste transportation. Over the past 18 years, an average of 200 commercial and federally owned spent fuel elements have been shipped per year. While there have been numerous accidents around the country involving non-radioactive hazardous materials, only six transportation accidents involving spent fuel casks have occurred since 1971 (when the federal requirement to report and record such incidents began). None of these accidents involved damage to the casks or the release of radiation to the public.

In spite of the excellent safety record for spent fuel transportation, there are few activities with such statistically low risks which arouse such intense public concern and media coverage. In addition, the number of nuclear-waste shipments will grow significantly with the operation of disposal and storage facilities, and transportation will proceed through more states and communities. The Congress recognized these concerns when enacting the NWPA, and directed DOE to take appropriate precautions to ensure the protection of public health and safety, and the environment, when conducting waste-management activities. The Congress further emphasized the need for public participation in DOE's planning to promote public confidence in the safety of waste disposal.

Development of the NWPA Transportation Program

We believe that significant progress has been made in the development of a transportation program that both meets these Congressional directives and satisfies many of the public concerns that form the basis of current legislative proposals.

THE COUNTERPOINT—by William L. Clay

In the interest of public safety there is a desperate need to develop a comprehensive federal policy governing the transportation of radioactive materials across our nation.

Public Safety at Risk

I've spent nearly two years monitoring the Department of Energy's shipment of irradiated fuel rods from Three Mile Island (TMI), Pennsylvania, to the Idaho National Engineering Laboratory (INEL) at Idaho Falls. I am convinced that the existing federal regulations governing such a transportation project fail to place a paramount importance on public safety.

In the case of DOE's TMI shipments, it appears that factors such as cost and expediency clearly outweighed the value of public safety. For example, the process of selecting a travel route for the TMI shipments was limited, according to the Department of Energy, because only one rail carrier serves TMI and only one rail carrier serves INEL. Accepting this constraint, the DOE purported to employ three criteria in evaluating the chosen route: quality of railroad track, avoidance of high population areas, and the quickest, most direct route. However, in fact, the only criteria on reflected in the route DOE selected was "quality of the track." The reality is, as my Missouri colleague Senator Danforth described it, that TMI shipments make "a beeline for large population centers."

Also, in the event that the TMI train derails or some other

accident occurs, the affected state and local governments are primarily responsible for initiating and monitoring the recovery operations. It is also the responsibility of each local government to gain the appropriate training and expertise for responding to such a nuclear accident. However, with regard to the TMI train shipments, there appears to be no federal requirement that the Department of Energy notify the affected communities that the shipment of radioactive material is moving through a community. In fact such notification has not always been made. I am also very concerned that many, if not most, local jurisdictions are not adequately equipped to respond to the kind of unforeseen disaster which could occur in connection with the Three Mile Island fuel core shipments.

Federal Laws Are Not Helping

In my experience the existing network of federal laws pertinent to the shipment of radioactive materials is so convoluted, fragmented, and wrought with ambiguity that it is extremely difficult if not impossible to effectively ensure my constituents that these transit projects conform to all the environmental protection and public safety requirements mandated by Congress.

For instance, one of the intentions of the Environmental Policy Act is that the federal government provide an Environmental Impact Statement (EIS) to accompany any major federal project that could significantly affect the human environment. In the case of the TMI shipments, there is no EIS. Instead, the Department of Energy is relying on a March 1981 programmatic Environmental Impact Statement which addresses the TMI site clean-up but does not address the matter of shipping spent fuel rods by railroad.

In addition, it has been my understanding that the intention of the Nuclear Waste Policy Act would require commercial irradiated nuclear fuel to be retained at a reactor site until a federal fuel repository is in operation, the utility company has paid all permanent disposal costs, and the Department of Energy has taken title to the fuel. These conditions have not been met in connection with the TMI project. Instead, the Department of Energy has devised an innovative policy to guide the transportation of spent nuclear fuel rods from Pennsylvania to Idaho which gives every appearance of violating the spirit if not the letter of this law.

Risks and Benefits

I began my study of the Department of Energy's TMI shipment project in an effort to understand whether the risk the public was assuming in allowing the government to move damaged radioactive materials through their cities and towns and farmlands was outweighed by the benefits which might be achieved. Unfortunately, two years later, I have a much better knowledge of the risk which is involved and almost no better knowledge of the benefits we might expect as a result of the Department of Energy's cross country shipment of damaged fuel core assemblies. The Department of Energy anticipates a better understanding of the nature of the failed fuel samples after they are reviewed by scientists at INEL. Unfortunately, this is a benefit which the layman, and even some scientists, see as vague and difficult to imagine and one which is readily obscured by the ominous and foreboding depiction of what we might imagine in the event that these TMI fuel rods find themselves in another accident. We must develop a holistic policy which ensures that the public benefit is in keeping with the public risk.

EXAMINING COUNTERPOINTS

This activity may be used as an individualized study guide for students in libraries and resource centers or as a discussion catalyst in small group and classroom discussions.

The Point

The nuclear waste repository program has made considerable progress. It recognizes the need for safe and permanent geologic disposal, and it has experienced very encouraging technical progress.

The Counterpoint

The nuclear waste repository program is a failure. It has been neither fair nor objective in the selection of a disposal site, and it has not provided reasonable assurances of safety and other benefits.

Guidelines

Part A

Examine the counterpoints above and then consider the following questions.

1. Do you agree more with the point or counterpoint? Why?

2. Which reading in this book best illustrates the point?

3. Which reading best illustrates the counterpoint?

4. Do any cartoons in this book illustrate the meaning of the point or counterpoint arguments? Which ones and why?

Part B

Social issues are usually complex, but often problems become over-simplified in political debates and discussions. Usually a polarized version of social conflict does not adequately represent the diversity of views that surround social conflicts. Examine the counterpoints. Then write down possible interpretations of this issue other than the two arguments stated in the counterpoints.

CHAPTER 4

DECOMMISSIONING NUCLEAR POWER PLANTS

14 DECOMMISSIONING NUCLEAR POWER PLANTS

DECOMMISSIONING NUCLEAR REACTORS IS FEASIBLE

Victor Stello

Victor Stello testified in his capacity as executive director for opera-tions at the U.S. Nuclear Regulatory Commission. He testified about decommissioning nuclear power plants, i.e., disposing of nuclear reactors and their radioactive waste.

Points to Consider:

1. What are the differences between the decommissioning of the Shippingport reactor and the decommissioning of large modern reactors? What are the similarities?

2. Describe the three decommissioning alternatives.

3. How much does the Nuclear Regulatory Commission es-timate it will cost to decommission a modern reactor?

Excerpted from the testimony of Victor Stello, April 23, 1987, before the House Subcommittee on Energy and Environment of the House Committee on Interior and Insular Affairs, April 23, 1987.

Conclusions indicated that decommissioning of modern reactors was feasible. Similar studies by the industry led to this same conclusion.

Decommissioning Is Feasible

While there have been no large reactors that have been decommissioned, our contractors, Battelle-Pacific Northwest Laboratory, did conceptual studies of the technology, safety and costs of decommissioning typical, modern pressurized water reactors and boiling water reactors. This was done using existing operating reactor experience during maintenance, actual decommissioning experience of smaller reactors, and practical extrapolation of existing technology. Their conclusion indicated that decommissioning of modern reactors was feasible. Similar studies by the industry led to this same conclusion.

The Navy Shippingport reactor is currently being decommissioned by the Department of Energy (DOE): The Nuclear Regulatory Commission (NRC), as part of its comprehensive program on reactor aging, is carefully documenting these activities in terms of decommissioning tasks, staff requirements, occupational exposures, and waste volume generation.

However, there are differences between the decommissioning of the Shippingport reactor and the decommissioning of large modern reactors.

Differences and Similarities

In the first case, the power output is smaller and the radioactivity is less than in a large modern reactor. Unlike what is expected to be done with commercial reactors, the Shippingport reactor pressure vessel is being removed intact instead of being segmented. In addition, the remaining radioactive waste is shipped to the Department of Energy waste burial grounds, which may have different acceptance criteria than NRC-licensed waste disposal facilities that commercial reactor licensees would be required to use.

On the other hand, there are many similarities between decommissioning the Shippingport reactor and decommissioning large commercial reactors. The physical size and complexity of systems of the Shippingport reactor are similar to large commercial reactors. Therefore, examination of the decommissioning activities in terms of tasks, staff requirements, occupational exposure, and waste volume generation can be used to develop information on parallel activities for large commercial reactors. The Shippingport decommissioning activities are well on their way and appear to be proceeding without major difficulties.

Dismantlement

There are three decommissioning alternatives that I would like to discuss today. The first alternative is dismantlement of a commercial nuclear power reactor. Dismantlement, which takes about six years, is a process whereby the radioactivity level of a reactor facility is reduced to a level that allows termination of the reactor license. This is accomplished through decontamination by chemical or mechanical means. In the latter case, the radioactive material is removed from the equipment, sometimes by cutting it into smaller pieces. These pieces are then packaged in a manner so that they can be sent to disposal facilities or to storage depending whether the pieces constitute low or high-level waste respectively.

A problem with dismantlement in the near future may be lack of waste disposal space, especially for the spent nuclear fuel rods since there are, as of this time, no high-level waste repositories. The majority of decommissioning waste is low level. For immediate dismantlement, the amount of low-level waste requiring disposal is about 18,000 cubic meters. But there are about 100 cubic meters of waste, per reactor, that are above Class C levels. These levels are not accepted by the commercial radioactive low-level waste burial grounds.

The 1985 amendments to the Low-Level Waste Policy Act require the federal government to take care of any special waste that cannot be disposed of in a low-level waste burial ground, but it is not high-level waste. The Department of Energy has disposal of such waste under consideration.

Safe Storage and Dismantlement

Under proposed NRC regulations, the second decommissioning alternative could be used: a reactor is made safe for storage and followed by dismantlement. A reactor could be maintained in safe storage, under NRC license, until such time that disposal space becomes available. This delay could have some advantage because, based on the Battelle-Pacific laboratory reports, most of the decommissioning waste is low-level waste that will, through decay, be reduced to one-tenth its volume after about 50 years and thereby result in a savings of low-level waste disposal space.

Moreover, radiation exposure can be significantly reduced by delays of 30 to 50 years.

Entombment

The third decommissioning alternative is entombment. With this alternative, the radioactive wastes are isolated from the environment by placing them in the hardened reactor containment building. Surveillance and maintenance are continued until, through decay, the radioactivity is reduced to an acceptable level.

For older reactors, long-lived radioactive niobium-94 and nickel-59 are generated through neutron activation primarily in the internal reactor systems. These have half-lives of 20,000 and 80,000 years respectively and would make consideration of entombment unreasonable.

However, removal of these internal reactor systems would allow consideration of entombment alternatives. Again, even for this configuration, decay of remaining radioactivity could take as long as 300 years, detracting from such entombment considerations.

Waste Disposal Costs

Decommissioning a modern reactor by dismantling is estimated to cost the utility about $100 to $130 million in 1986 dollars. In terms of decommissioning activities, this refers only

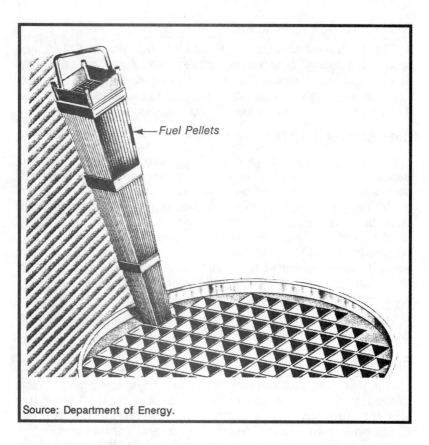

Fuel Pellets

Source: Department of Energy.

to those activities that involve the removal of radioactivity which is above an acceptable level, thus allowing for unrestricted release of the facility and termination of the NRC license.

Such items as the cost of demolition and removal of non-radioactive structures or buildings, or the restoration of the site are not included in our estimated cost. Other items that are traditionally handled as part of operational cost, are already covered under existing regulations and are not included in the NRC decommissioning cost requirements. The additional costs associated with these type of activities are difficult to project, but it may be a substantial increase to the $100 to $130 million estimate. . . .

Various Decommissioning Activities

As I mentioned earlier, during the decommissioning of the Shippingport reactor, the NRC has been working with DOE to obtain information on various decommissioning activities in terms of staff requirements, occupational exposures, the quantity and type of radioactive waste generated and its appropriate classification for commercial low-level and high-level waste burial. We are also characterizing the nature and distribution of radiation in and around the reactor, as well as the type of long-term radioactive materials that must be dealt with. . . .

Future research efforts include continued monitoring of the Shippingport activities, as well as keeping abreast of any potential decommissioning activities that may have generic value such as the possible dismantlement of a large commercial reactor.

15 DECOMMISSIONING NUCLEAR POWER PLANTS

QUESTIONS OF DISMANTLING REACTORS STILL UNANSWERED

Cynthia Pollock

Cynthia Pollock testified on behalf of the Worldwatch Institute, an independent, nonprofit research organization based in Washington, D.C. Worldwatch was established to inform policymakers and the general public about the interdependence of the world economy and its environmental support systems.

Points to Consider:

1. What is Shippingport? How much will it cost to decommission Shippingport?

2. Why does the author believe that decommissioning costs are likely to increase?

3. Of the four retired commercial reactors in the United States, how many had begun to build a decommissioning fund before shutting down?

4. Explain why the author recommends using a large reactor as an international test case.

Excerpted from the testimony of Cynthia Pollock before the House Subcommittee on Energy and Environment of the House Committee on Interior and Insular Affairs, April 23, 1987.

Thirty years after Shippingport—the first U.S. power reactor—entered service, the question of how to safely and economically dispose of nuclear reactors and their wastes is still largely unanswered.

Although nuclear power supplied 15 percent of the nation's electricity last year, not a single large commercial unit has ever been dismantled anywhere in the world. Assuming a 30-year operating license, 70 U.S. reactors will be taken out of service by 2010. That's just 23 years from now.

The Cost of Decommissioning

There are many unknowns surrounding decommissioning, the biggest of which is probably its cost. Cost estimates are highly speculative and range from $100 million to $3 billion per reactor. The latter figure equals the average cost of building a modern U.S. facility. Lack of decommissioning experience makes it impossible to know if current estimates are on target.

The experience of decommissioning the Shippingport reactor is not likely to provide many clues. It is a reactor with one-fifteenth of the generating capacity of large modern reactors. The unit was decontaminated during its operating life, and doesn't require decontamination as part of decommissioning. The reactor had several cores, and it's a facility with a unique transportation arrangement that avoids the expensive and difficult task of dismantling the pressure vessel that will be required at larger reactors.

Despite all of these cost-saving characteristics, decommissioning Shippingport is projected to cost $98 million. This is $1.36 million per megawatt, the equivalent of $1.5 billion for an 1100-megawatt reactor.

While the legitimacy of scaling up costs is questionable, there are many factors that are likely to push up future decommissioning costs.

Other Cost Considerations

For example, the cost of simply decontaminating, not dismantling, the Dresden Unit 1 in Illinois, a 210-megawatt reactor that operated for only 18 years, was $40 million. That's just for chemical and physical cleanup.

In addition, dismantling a 1,100-megawatt pressurized water reactor will produce 18,000 cubic meters of contaminated concrete and steel, one and one-half times as much as was produced during the plant's 30-year operating life, or enough to bury a football field 12-feet deep.

Boiling water reactors, of which there are almost 40 in the United States, produce an even greater amount of contaminated debris. And as we've just heard, the cost of shallow land burial of low-level waste has increased more than 19-fold during the last decade.

The three sites currently accepting low-level waste will soon close and regional compacts established in compliance with the Low-Level Radioactive Waste Policy Act have yet to decide upon new sites.

It is also apparent that the compacts are not including in the decisionmaking process the large volumes of waste that will result from decommissioning. Dismantling just one reactor will produce one-quarter as much waste as is currently sent to all three low-level waste sites during an entire year.

Decommissioning Costs Likely to Increase

One thing is certain. The problems inherent in establishing new waste facilities, particularly those with superior technologies and stricter regulations, will further boost decommissioning costs.

As decommissioning experience is gained, new and stricter

regulations will also probably be put into place that will likely increase costs. For example, residual radioactivity standards have not yet been promulgated by the Environmental Protection Agency, so utilities don't know how clean they have to leave their sites. Nor are there regulations that specify which wastes are considered to be contaminated and therefore require disposal in a low-level waste site.

Another area of uncertainty revolves around transuranic wastes. The Department of Energy (DOE) has been made responsible for disposal of these highly radioactive elements, but it hasn't yet decided which method of disposal it will use. Deep geologic disposal, the most likely option, will be many more times more expensive than shallow-land burial.

Further complicating the development of cost estimates is the likelihood that economies of scale and the benefits of the learning curve may not be as great as anticipated. This has certainly been the case as far as construction costs go, and since most reactors in the United States are basically custom built instead of by standardized design, experience gained at one plant site may not be directly transferable to another. The degree of contamination will also vary from reactor to reactor and will depend on how well the plant was operated. The more fuel leaks experienced at a reactor, the more contaminated it will be.

Other elements which could increase costs are if the plants are stored for many years, thereby requiring substantial security costs, and also the loss of staff with the best knowledge of the plant.

Some Decommissioning Recommendations

I will now briefly outline some recommendations for making us better prepared for nuclear power plant decommissioning.

First, we need to resolve the dilemma of where to dispose of high-level nuclear waste. Despite the best of efforts, spent fuel disposal policy appears to be unraveling. Until either a high-level waste repository or a monitored retrievable storage facility is established, decommissioning policy will be held hostage to the lack of disposal sites. Dismantlement will not be possible. DOE must be made to abide in good faith with the Nuclear Waste Policy Act.

Second, the Nuclear Regulatory Commission must issue decommissioning guidelines so that utilities can plan accordingly.

"I SAY LET'S BUILD IT... IF IT FAILS TO GET A LICENSE WE CAN CONVERT IT INTO A POOR HOUSE FOR CUSTOMERS WHO WOULD GO BROKE PAYING FOR IT!"

Cartoon by Wayne Stayskal. Reprinted by permission: Tribune Media Services.

I submit that these guidelines should require external savings accounts managed by professional investors and composed of diversified assets. At least ten states now require this method of funding by the nuclear utilities in order to assure that funds will be available when needed. Even this method would not be sufficient if the reactor is retired earlier than expected. . . . Of the four retired commercial reactors in the United States, only one unit had begun to build a decommissioning fund before it shut down. The Pacific Gas & Electric Co., owner of the Humboldt Bay reactor, collected $500,000 during the four years prior to plant closure. The amount is less than 1 percent of what the company estimates it will cost to decommission the reactor.

I would also suggest that entombment should not be considered an option for power reactors because it is impossible that all contaminants would decay to levels permissible for unrestricted use within a period of 100 years.

In addition, I'll make it unanimous that we all agree a minimum funding level should be substantially higher than $100 million, with provisions for periodic review of the reasonableness of this amount included in the regulations. There should also be a requirement for plant-specific, as opposed to generic, cost estimates. As we have heard, costs vary greatly, depending on plant design, the manner in which it was operated, and various aspects unique to specific reactors, such as geography of the area, size of the containment structure, etc.

The California Public Utility Commission recently decided that $579 million was a reasonable estimate for the two-unit, 2,200-megawatt Diablo Canyon plant, and Arkansas Power and Light plans to propose a $350 million to $400 million fund for its two-unit 1,700-megawatt plant in Russellville. As we have heard, the analysts working for the Atomic Industrial Forum are also proposing costs of $250 million per reactor and have been quoted as calling current estimates a "crapshoot."

As I outlined earlier, there are many factors that are likely to further increase decommissioning costs. Perhaps most startling and foreboding is an estimate made by Bechtel International for dismantling a clean 700-megawatt reactor in Austria that was never loaded with fuel and therefore, not contaminated. The company projected that a complete demolition would take about seven years and cost $105 million for a clean plant.

More Recommendations

The third recommendation I have is that Environmental Protection Agency needs to issue residual radioactivity guidelines so utilities will know the extent of the clean-up effort required.

Fourth, states need to plan for future low-level waste sites with the large volumes of decommissioning debris in mind.

Fifth, the Nuclear Regulatory Commission, DOE, International Atomic Energy Agency, Nuclear Energy Agency, and private groups need to conduct more research and development on decommissioning. This includes work on remotely controlled technologies, dust suppression systems, decontamination and disposal practices, and waste volume reduction techniques. This information must be freely shared with utilities and local, state, and national governments.

Sixth, a large reactor that has operated for many years should be dismantled as an international test case. Current decommissioning programs focus only on small reactors with short operating lives. These are much less relevant to future needs because radiation builds up in proportion to the plant's capacity multiplied by the number of years it has operated.

Costs could be shared among the reactor owner and interested governments and research institutes from around the world. The United Kingdom, the Soviet Union, and the United States, as the pioneers of nuclear power, each have reactors sufficiently large and contaminated to serve the purpose.

RECOGNIZING AUTHOR'S POINT OF VIEW

This activity may be used as an individualized study guide for students in libraries and resource centers or as a discussion catalyst in small group and classroom discussions.

The capacity to recognize an author's point of view is an essential reading skill. Many readers do not make clear distinctions between descriptive articles that relate factual information and articles that express a point of view. Think about the readings in Chapter Four. Are these readings essentially descriptive articles that relate factual information or articles that attempt to persuade through editorial commentary and analysis?

Guidelines

1. Read through the following source descriptions. Choose one of the source descriptions that best describes each reading in Chapter Four.

    ### Source Descriptions

    a. Essentially an article that relates factual information
    b. Essentially an article that expresses editorial points of view
    c. Both of the above
    d. None of the above

2. After careful consideration, pick out one source that you agree with the most. Be prepared to explain the reasons for your choice in a general class discussion.

CHAPTER 5

THE NUCLEAR WEAPONS COMPLEX

16 THE NUCLEAR WEAPONS COMPLEX

MODERNIZING NUCLEAR WEAPONS PRODUCTION

The Department of Energy

This reading is excerpted from the United States Department of Energy Nuclear Weapons Complex Modernization Report, *a study directed by Congress in recognition of a comprehensive approach to address the problems surrounding the Nuclear Weapons Complex.*

Points to Consider:

1. Why does the Nuclear Weapons Complex need to be modernized?

2. What are the principal requirements for modernizing the Complex?

3. Describe the key modernization actions.

4. How much will modernization and environmental restoration cost?

Excerpted from the *United States Department of Energy Nuclear Weapons Complex Modernization Report,* Report to the Congress by the President, December 1980.

The modernized Complex will be more streamlined and cost effective with the flexibility to adapt to a broad spectrum of potential military, political, and technological futures.

The Nuclear Weapons Complex (Complex) of the U.S. Department of Energy (DOE) provides the nuclear weapons that support the nuclear deterrent policy. This support includes production of nuclear material; design and manufacture of nuclear weapons; surveillance and maintenance of nuclear weapons in the stockpile; research, development, and testing of nuclear devices; and modernization of the nuclear weapons stockpile.

A Major, Long-term Modernization Effort

Much of the Complex was constructed more than 30 years ago. Some facilities are experiencing operability problems due to obsolete equipment and operational systems and to stresses in complying with more stringent environmental, safety, and health standards and requirements. Many facilities throughout the Complex are approaching the end of their useful lives. For example, the existing production reactors, at their current power limits, have limited operational capability. All three reactors are shut down for safety system improvements and are not expected to be fully operational until late 1989. In spite of these improvements and increasingly extensive maintenance, the reactors may not be able to achieve acceptable production efficiencies. Other elements of the Complex, as discussed in the report, are approaching a critical state similar to that of the production reactors. Correcting these inadequacies and placing these operations in an exemplary condition will require the support by both the Congress and the Administration for a major, long-term modernization effort.

A Modernization Plan

The Congress recognized that a comprehensive (instead of piecemeal) approach was needed to address these problems, and directed that a study be conducted and a plan prepared by the President ". . .for the modernization of the Nuclear Weapons Complex that takes into account the overall size, productive capacity, technology base, and investment strategy necessary to support long-term national security objectives." The study has been completed and a Modernization Plan (Plan) has been prepared.

The study shows that the entire Complex will require extensive modernization over the next 15-20 years to meet its obligations well into the next century. The principal requirements central to the need for modernizing the Complex are:

- Meeting the Department of Defense (DOD) requirements for modern nuclear weapons stockpile;

- Maintaining nuclear weapons technological superiority;

- Complying with environmental, safety, and health requirements; and

- Providing the flexibility to adapt to changing production and technological needs with minimum impact on schedules and cost.

A More Streamlined and Cost Effective Complex

To meet these requirements, the Complex must retain all of its primary functions but must undergo several major modifications to its infrastructure. New production reactor capacity will be provided with the preferred sites being the Savannah River Plant and the Idaho National Engineering Laboratory. A Special Isotope Separation Plant is expected to be constructed at the Idaho National Engineering Laboratory to convert DOE inventories of fuel-grade plutonium into weapon-grade plutonium. Nuclear material operations will be consolidated to the extent that efficiency, environmental, or safety aspects of the operation can be improved and transportation of nuclear materials can be minimized. The most significant physical changes will be the relocation of all operations from the Rocky Flats Plant to other DOE facilities and the termination of Nuclear Materials Production activities at the Hanford Plant and at the Fernald Feed Materials Production Center. Nuclear materials activities at the Mound Plant will be transferred to existing DOE facilities that have nuclear materials operations. Waste Management and Environmental Restoration activities at these sites will continue until completion. Designing and testing of new weapons concepts, certification of the safety and reliability of the nuclear weapons stockpile, and applied research will continue to be performed by the three nuclear weapons laboratories.

The modernized Complex will be more streamlined and cost effective with the flexibility to adapt to a broad spectrum of potential military, political, and technological futures. The resulting Complex will meet all applicable standards for protection of the environment and of the safety and health of employees and the public.

Key Modernization Actions

The key modernization actions are prioritized into three categories:

- Those actions that are time-critical and essential for current operations;
- Those actions essential for continued operations; and
- Those actions needed to optimize the Complex for the future.

Figure 1 summarizes the prioritized modernization activities identified in the Plan and shows their tentative implementation schedules. In addition, key short-term activities, important in the transition period before modernization is completed, are addressed in the Plan.

In developing a Resource Plan for modernization, all future demands for resources by the Complex were considered,

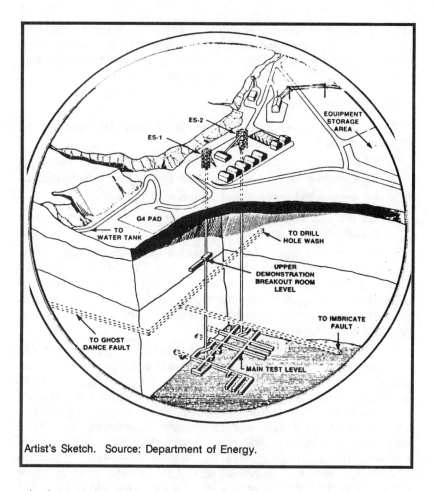

Artist's Sketch.   Source: Department of Energy.

whether or not they could be directly related to modernization of the Complex. Inclusion of all resources is not intended to provide a "twenty-year budget," but to recognize that competition for funding will require difficult tradeoffs and prioritization of all programs. An example is the Environmental Restoration program which includes environmental cleanup and decontamination and decommissioning of inactive facilities; although not a modernization activity per se, the costs of the Environmental Restoration activities are inescapable consequences of modernization.

Specific annual funding profiles for accomplishing the modernization activities in this Plan are not included since such funding must be considered in the context of the total national security requirements in any given year. While the budget for Fiscal Year (FY) 1990 will be generally consistent with this Plan, accomplishing all recommendations of the Plan in the timeframe specified will require resources greater than those now expected to be available in future years. Thus, schedules shown in this document must be regarded as tentative.

Major Modernization Issues

The major modernization issues that must be resolved to implement this Plan effectively are:

- The timing and level of sustained resources required independent of fluctuating annual production requirements;
- Environmental, safety, and health issues; and
- Issues associated with relocations, consolidations, and transportation.

The estimated cost* for modernization and environmental restoration for the period FY 1990 through FY 2010 is about $81 billion; about $52 billion is associated with modernization. A breakdown by activity of the cumulative modernization and environmental restoration incremental costs for the 21-year period are shown in Figure 2.

Present and future operation of the Complex will require environmental, safety, and health corrective actions and a base program to ensure that these operations comply with applicable laws, standards, and regulations. These actions are separate from environmental restoration activities. Evolving regulations and standards and their application and differences in regional and state approaches will require realistic strategies that are consistently applied across the entire Complex. Funding constraints and our technical ability to achieve cost-effective compliance in facilities that are 30 or more years old dictate that a realistic schedule be established to replace or upgrade our facilities. As new facilities are built or existing facilities are upgraded for programmatic reasons, reviews will be conducted

---

*The costs presented in the resource plan are not budget quality, but rather first-level approximations for use in identifying future trends and levels of effort. The cost of modernization in this report is expressed as the increment above the FY 1989 appropriated level summed over the 21-year period, FY 1990 through FY 2010. All dollar figures are expressed in constant FY 1990 dollars. The FY 1989 appropriated level expressed in FY 1990 dollars is $7.8 billion. All estimates exclude funding for the Naval reactors program.

to ensure that state-of-the-art technology is provided to protect the environment and the safety and health of workers and the public. Approximately $25 billion will be required over the next 20 years for the environmental, safety, and health base program and corrective actions.** This corresponds to a total increase of $3.0 billion above the FY 1989 appropriation level accumulated over the 21-year period.

Apart from modernization, the cleanup and environmental restoration of the various sites present a technological and financial challenge that may dictate the degree and timing of this activity. The rate of increase and the level of funding can be adjusted to accommodate national priorities.

Major environmental restoration will be required at the Rocky Flats, Hanford, and Fernald sites when the Nuclear Weapons Complex activities are either relocated or terminated. As an interim program, certain upgrades will be required at the Rocky Flats Plant to maintain operations at an acceptable level of risk while the relocated facilities are being constructed.

Both the Administration and Congress recognize the need for the actions set forth in this report; expeditious implementation of the proposed Plan is recommended.

**This amount is included in the funding for the major programs listed in Section 2 and should not be added separately.

17 THE NUCLEAR WEAPONS COMPLEX

CLOSING DOWN THE BOMB FACTORIES

The Militant

This reading originally appeared as an editorial in The Militant, *a socialist newsweekly.*

Points to Consider:

1. How many nuclear weapons production plants have been pouring radioactive and other toxic wastes into the environment?

2. Describe the Department of Energy's proposed solutions.

3. Which plant has caused the most serious environmental damage? What kind of damage has occurred?

4. What happened when Soviet President Mikhail Gorbachev urged the U.S. government to reduce nuclear weapons?

"Government Wants $45 Billion to Keep Nuclear Arsenal," *The Militant,* December 23, 1988.

U.S. nuclear weapons plants must be shut down for good, and the nuclear stockpiles destroyed. All commercial nuclear reactors should be shut down too.

The trickle of revelations has become a flood. An environmental disaster, perpetrated by the U.S. government, is taking place at nuclear weapons production plants across the country.

The 12 plants have poured radioactive and other toxic wastes into the environment. Nuclear accidents, radioactive emissions, and toxic dumping have been knowingly concealed from the public.

A Deadly Course

The damage to the health of workers inside the weapons plants has yet to be accurately gauged and made public. "Many occupational health professionals say it is impossible to draw any conclusions about the health of the nuclear workers," reported the December 11 *New York Times*, "because the Federal Occupational Safety and Health Administration has no power in the plants, because security rules have limited the access of union officials and other safety inspectors, and because the Energy Department will not release for independent review the health records on which [its] studies are based."

This deadly course was pursued by Washington over decades — regardless of whether it was a Republican or Democrat who sat in the White House Oval Office, whether it was Republicans or Democrats who headed congressional "oversight" committees.

Proposed Solutions

Now the Department of Energy has come up with its proposed solutions. The central objective: to keep the weapons of mass death coming off the production line, no matter what the cost in human health, environmental destruction, and financial resources.

The Department of Energy proposes spending $45 billion to build new nuclear weapons plants to replace some of the old, deteriorating, and now widely discredited plants. As the proposals were being made public, the *New York Times* reported that the agency has spent more than $5 billion since 1970 on nuclear power projects that had to be abandoned.

In addition to calling for new plants, the DOE insists that

"national security" requires that one of the reactors shut down for safety reasons at the Savannah River plant in South Carolina must quickly be brought back on line to produce tritium. Otherwise, officials warn, some of the thousands of nuclear bombs may have to be dismantled. Officials concede that the plant will not meet the DOE's safety standards when it starts up.

Tritium, a key radioactive component of many nuclear weapons, decays at a rate of 5.5 percent annually. The tritium has to be replaced periodically or else the weapons must be junked.

Details and Priorities

When details concerning what measures to take and how much to spend are being debated in Congress, there is a broad consensus in ruling circles on priorities. An editorial in the December 9 *Times* cited three problems facing the weapons makers: "production capacity, environmental cleanup, and long-term nuclear waste disposal."

"The first," the editors insisted, "is by far the most urgent."

The needs of U.S. working people are radically different. Our interests require shutting down the weapons-making system now.

Environmental Hazards

The latest admissions from the DOE came December 6, when the agency issued a ranking of environmental hazards at the plants.

The most serious damage, the DOE now admits, took place at the Rocky Flats plant, a few miles from Denver. Toxic wastes from the plant have been leaking into underground water supplies and have already contaminated the soil in the surrounding area.

A successful suit by local landholders forced the release of documents. They revealed, according to the December 12 *Washington Post,* that "in just over 35 years of operation, Rocky Flats has experienced hundreds of small fires and at least two major blazes that likely involved significant radioactivity releases."

Public health officials believe that the plutonium dust contaminating the land surrounding the plant has been carried far from there by the wind: Environmentalists termed the situation "a creeping Chernobyl."

Contaminated Sites

The DOE describes the Idaho National Engineering Laboratory near Idaho Falls as one of the most contaminated sites in the weapons industry. Operations there discharged radioactive and toxic wastes into disposal lagoons and wells that have contaminated the Snake River aquifer— the principal water source for eastern Idaho.

The DOE says that $110 billion will be needed over the long term to repair and limit the damage already caused by the nuclear weapons production plants.

The DOE is requesting another $30 billion to process and store the nuclear wastes that have been produced by the plants, and up to $10 billion to attempt to decontaminate and dismantle several hundred unusable facilities.

The recently completed storage center in Carlsbad, New Mexico, which was scheduled to open last October, is riddled with leaks into the surrounding groundwater. The opening of the center, once portrayed as a leak-proof answer to the waste storage problem, has now been put off indefinitely.

This is the price—the enormous human, environmental, and financial price—that the people of the United States and the world will be forced to pay as long as Washington is committed to maintaining its nuclear arsenal. There's no such thing as safe production of nuclear weapons.

Reducing Nuclear Weapons

Soviet President Mikhail Gorbachev, in his December 7, 1988 speech to the United National General Assembly, announced that the Soviet government would unilaterally reduce its armed

CAMPAIGN FOR GLOBAL SECURITY

SANE/FREEZE

CLOSE NUCLEAR WEAPONS PLANTS PERMANENTLY

KEEP THEM SHUT

711 G ST. SE, WASHINGTON DC 20003

forces by 500,000—about 10 percent of the total—and withdraw 50,000 troops and 5,000 tanks from countries in Eastern Europe.

He also urged the U.S. government to join in agreements to reduce nuclear weapons by 50 percent and to eliminate chemical weapons.

President Ronald Reagan insisted the next day that significant U.S. cuts "can't happen with our defense spending until we have reached a parity."

Gorbachev's initiative increased the pressure on the U.S. rulers and their allies in Europe, and heightened debate in Congress and the U.S. big-business media over reducing U.S. arms spending as part of efforts to limit the government's budget deficit.

Nonetheless the administration is seeking to rally bipartisan support in Congress for spending tens of billions to refurbish the nuclear weapons plants and create new ones. New plants, we are promised, will be immune to leaks and other disasters—just as the current ones were said to be not too long ago.

Soviet Offer Provides an Opening

The Soviet government's offer to cut its troop strength in Europe provides an opening to demand that Washington withdraw all its troops, nuclear weapons, tanks, and other military hardware from Europe now.

- U.S. nuclear weapons plants must be shut down for good as well, and the nuclear stockpiles destroyed. All commercial nuclear reactors should be shut down too.

- The billions now spent on the U.S. military budget should be used instead to meet the needs of working people. High on the list are massive programs to repair the environmental damage done by nuclear plants, work toward a solution to the problem of nuclear waste disposal, and provide the free health care that workers at nuclear plants and millions of people who have lived in harm's way are entitled to.

18 THE NUCLEAR WEAPONS COMPLEX

PROGRESS IN DOE SAFETY PROCEDURES

Mary L. Walker

Mary L. Walker testified in her capacity as assistant secretary for Environment, Safety, and Health of the United States Department of Energy.

Points to Consider:

1. Describe the Department's safety goal.

2. How has the safety oversight system been applied in the past?

3. What further actions is the Department taking to improve safety?

Excerpted from the testimony of Mary L. Walker before the House Subcommittee on Oversight and Investigations of the House Committee on Energy and Commerce, October 22, 1987.

Now that we are beginning to understand the full scope of the issues that confront the Department, it is fair to ask what we have done, and what we are doing to address them. . . . Let me assure you that while much remains to be done, things are better.

In the environmental area, significant progress has been achieved in resolving longstanding issues of noncompliance at our sites through strong compliance agreements with the Environmental Protection Agency and the states. In addition to immediate corrective actions taken to mitigate known pollutant sources, the Environmental Survey is providing a better understanding of existing on-site contamination which will form the basis for long-term remedial action.

The Goal: Excellence in Safety

The fact that the Department's nuclear facilities are aging—most date to the 1950s with some built during World War II—is well-known. The question of their adequacy, in the context of safety, is much more complex, involving changing public expectations, evolving regulatory criteria, maturing technology, and the inevitable comparisons of practices at the Department of Energy (DOE) and Nuclear Regulatory Commission (NRC). The goal of our oversight program is not just to achieve compliance, but in keeping with the Secretary's policy, to strive for excellence in operations as a means to enhance safe operation.

The imperative for excellence in safety has been well recognized in the wake of Chernobyl and the Challenger tragedy, and more recently in other technological facets of everyday life such as railway operations and commercial aviation. If there is a common denominator to this experience, it is that both conservative safety design and the "human element" continue to be critical considerations. In nuclear safety, we should have no patience with inadequate safety design, incomplete or unclear procedures, failure to follow procedures, or even complacency born of a good record. Pursuing excellence in safety is not a mere goal or standard; it represents an attitude and a workplace culture that we see as one of the strongest means to minimize the likelihood of severe accidents.

The Technical Safety Appraisals performed by my office were designed to bring an independent, wide range of nuclear safety technical expertise to bear on each of our nuclear facilities, and to evaluate operations comprehensively and independently at

129

AN IMPLEMENTATION PLAN

Michael J. Lawrence, Manager of the Department of Energy's (DOE) Richland Operations Office, today directed that statements of needs raised in a DOE review of three Rockwell Hanford Operations internal audits be transmitted to the contractor and that Rockwell prepare an implementation plan for meeting those needs by December 12.

In taking the action, Lawrence said:

"I believe our facilities have been operated in a safe and responsible manner and our operating systems provide a wide margin of safety. In addition, the DOE Headquarters, Operations Offices and Contractor safety and quality assurance system work as evidenced by the strong actions taken to correct deficiencies. However, the lack of discipline, the failure to correct the causes of problems addressed and ill-defined procedures reduced the margin of safety built into our operational process. This is unacceptable. The Department and its contractors must take every step to insure continued safety and safety reviews." Such a step was taken on October 8 when plutonium handling inspections at two of our processing facilities were halted.

Excerpted from the testimony of Michael J. Lawrence before the House Subcommittee on Oversight and Investigations of the House Committee on Energy and Commerce, May 11, 1988

those facilities against today's standards. Where uncertainties or key technical issues have been raised, the Department has been a strong advocate for safety, and operations at the Department have, where appropriate, been either suspended or modified. . . .

Safety Oversight System Has Not Always Worked Effectively

This aggressive oversight, this attention to the letter and spirit of environment and safety compliance, has not been consistently applied in the past. When he joined the Department, Secretary Herrington found inadequate attention to safety and weakened oversight. It was his resolve, in 1985, to reverse this situation through initiatives—and a change in direction—that have strengthened environmental and safety oversight. . . .

The symptoms of this condition have become more evident during the course of the Department's appraisal programs and evaluations. The record of worker safety has remained good relative to National Safety Council statistics, however progress in reducing nuclear accident risks has not kept pace with that of the commercial sector; some nuclear safety standards have not uniformly been made comparable or effectively enforced in the past; some aging facilities are overdue for replacement or major refurbishment; and the compliance system used to assure contractors and DOE line management compliance with good practices did not posses the rigor and accountability that should be demanded of nuclear operations.

Further Actions Are Being Taken

Now that we are beginning to understand the full scope of the issues that confront the Department, it is fair to ask what we have done, and what we are doing to address them. . . .

In radiation protection, for example, specialists in radiation monitoring have identified improvements in technology and measurement practice that will enhance our ability to assure radiation exposure is maintained as low as reasonably achievable. In fire protection, the longstanding use of casualty experts from Factory Mutual and Schrimer have served to surface a number of key findings on how the Department's fire protection and referenced building codes are implemented. This is enabling both my office and the Operations Offices to address these issues in a deliberate fashion through better standards implementation, compliance oversight, and inspections.

Another initiative the Department is pursuing is the establishment of contractor self-improvement or "excellence" programs in nuclear safety. One lesson that came from the Three Mile Island accident was that regulatory oversight, by itself, does not assure safe operation. What is needed from an institutional sense is a proactive and dynamic approach for instilling safety excellence at the working level, which in DOE's case is the operating contractor. . . .

Conclusion

The last two years have been a time of needed introspection on the part of the Department with respect to its nuclear safety program—its standards, oversight, and credibility. The Secretary has made this an open process from the beginning. As a result, while gaining us the advantage of the broadest perspectives on the issues before us, the surfacing of these same issues has

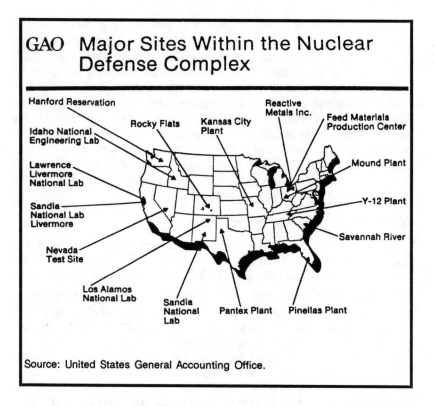

GAO Major Sites Within the Nuclear Defense Complex

Hanford Reservation

Idaho National Engineering Lab

Lawrence Livermore National Lab

Sandia National Lab Livermore

Nevada Test Site

Los Alamos National Lab

Rocky Flats

Kansas City Plant

Sandia National Lab

Pantex Plant

Pinellas Plant

Reactive Metals Inc.

Feed Materials Production Center

Mound Plant

Y-12 Plant

Savannah River

Source: United States General Accounting Office.

served to feed the perception that the safety program is growing worse, not better.

Let me assure you that while much remains to be done, things are better. The acknowledgment that the safety function and oversight system in DOE has not always been as effective as it should have been represents a dramatic break with the past—one that now allows us to determine how best to improve upon what is not working effectively, while preserving the best features of a program that has still produced one of the best safety records in the industry. As before, we welcome the perspectives and findings of outside reviewers on what institutional and facility safety issues need to be addressed by DOE. The National Academies of Science and Engineering review requested by Secretary Herrington of our production reactors is in the process of being completed. Their recommendations, expected shortly, will help guide our future efforts.

The Department's goal has been to translate recognized problems into actions, and actions into institutional solutions.

We recognize that in order to effectively accomplish the Department's missions, we must demonstrate that DOE is a credible guardian of the environment in which its operations are conducted, and that the public and workers' safety and health can be adequately assured. Change has occurred, and still more changes will occur, as we continue to implement Secretary Herrington's call for excellence. In so doing, we recognize as we have previously testified, that the Department of Energy's critical missions must not be jeopardized by an environmental and safety program too weak to assure excellence, or by one so rigid and oppressive that its missions cannot be accomplished effectively.

19 THE NUCLEAR WEAPONS COMPLEX

A SAFETY PROGRAM IN SHAMBLES

U.S. House of Representatives Subcommittee on Oversight and Investigations

This reading is excerpted from a memorandum written by the Sub-committee staff to the Subcommittee chairman regarding health and safety at Department of Energy nuclear weapons facilities.

Points to Consider:

1. Describe the safety problems that exist at weapons facilities.

2. What is a criticality incident?

3. How have serious safety problems been covered up?

4. Why has the DOE not been completely candid about its safety problems? What are the root causes of DOE's safety problems?

Excerpted from the testimony of the Subcommittee on Oversight and Investigations of the House Committee on Energy and Commerce, October 22, 1987.

In an attempt to look good, DOE has hurt its health and safety program by not being completely candid with itself and outsiders.

Based on its ongoing investigation of safety at DOE nuclear weapons plants, the Subcommittee staff has found that the safety program at DOE is not working effectively. We visited the Hanford site last March and the Savannah River Plant in August. DOE and contractor safety appraisals and audits, as well as reports prepared by outside consultants, have been reviewed. We also talked with many individuals, ranging from top DOE and contractor managers to plant safety workers.

We selected Hanford, Savannah River, and Albuquerque for study. In some cases, we found the same problems existing at each location. Because these are among the DOE's largest and most important activities, there may be a serious breakdown in the entire DOE safety program.

There is a striking similarity between our review of safety and the Subcommittee's five-year, continuing investigation into the adequacy of safeguards and security at the DOE's nuclear weapons production complex. Inadequate safeguards and security, which could have resulted in the theft of bomb-grade nuclear materials, were attributed to an "it-can't-happen-here" attitude; bureaucratic infighting; the existence of a "good ole boy" network and "buddy bonus" system; and an inverse "rewards and punishment" system that rewards those who hide serious problems and punishes those who attempt to expose serious problems. We believe these same factors contribute to a serious safety situation at the nuclear weapons production complex.

DOE's Safety Program in Shambles

Major safety problems have been found to exist at the weapons facilities. These problems range from those that can cause instant damage—fires and critical incidents—to those that do their damage over long periods of time, such as unnecessary exposure of workers to radiation. Even the program designed to increase the chances that things will not go wrong—Quality Assurance—has deteriorated.

Here are some examples of what we found:

- A major fire at a nuclear facility could kill and injure many people, contaminate the environment with radioactivity, and disrupt vital defense programs. DuPont at the Savannah

River Plant adopted a corporate philosophy that fire protection is really unnecessary because they believe fires can be prevented. This has resulted in fire protection being practically nonexistent. Even the DOE, in 1986, warned that a major fire may occur because basic fire protection program elements are not in place. Things have been so bad that the only thing available to fight a fire at a reactor building was an ordinary garden hose. Automatic sprinkler systems were deliberately not turned on at the one-of-a-kind Tritium Facility because a DuPont manager was more concerned about computers, electrical components, and paper records getting wet than the Tritium Facility burning down. Also, at one critical facility, the operations people instruct the fire department on how to fight a fire. Other fire problems found were lack of fire protection water supply, lack of automatic fire extinguishing systems, and lack of prompt fire department response capability.

- One of the worst things that can happen at a nuclear facility is to have a criticality incident, which is an unplanned and uncontrolled nuclear reaction. Intense radiation is released, which can kill personnel within seconds. At the Plutonium Finishing and PUREX Plants at Hanford, over 50 Criticality Specification Violations have occurred over the past several years. In spite of the incredible potential for a major criticality accident as a result of these violations, DOE did not stop operations until October 1986, after intense interest in safety at Hanford was aroused by the media and by the Subcommittee.

- Workers assigned to perform critical tasks affecting the safety of DOE nuclear plants must be properly trained or certified. Unqualified people in critical safety positions can pose a significant risk to the safety of the nuclear weapons program.

Albuquerque contractors were not properly following the departmental procedures for training and certifying nuclear operators and for keeping them current by retraining and recertifying them. Several safety-related inspectors at the N Reactor had not been properly certified for their jobs because of improperly-graded tests and inadequate experience. It was not until much later, approximately five years, that the mistake was found. In the meantime, four inspectors, who actually flunked their tests, were allowed to conduct critical safety inspections at the N Reactor. Also, non-certified personnel performed inspections of critical reactor systems at the Savannah River production reactors.

- Workers at nuclear weapons plants are exposed to extreme hazards. It is imperative for their health and safety that every possible measure be taken to protect them from harm. DOE has not been successful in protecting their workers from harm. . . .

DOE has a policy that radiation exposure to workers be kept as low as reasonably achievable (ALARA). This policy has been deliberately violated. At the N Reactor, workers were purposely exposed to the absolute maximum dose of 500 millirems (MR) per week, even though the normal maximum exposure rate is only 300 MR per week. The ALARA policy was being violated because of production pressures. Contractor supervisory personnel were certifying, in advance, that no other qualified workers were available, even before they had knowledge of any programmatic need to exceed the ALARA 300 MR level. . . .

Serious Safety Problems Are Covered Up

Unless health and safety problems are reported in an honest and timely manner, it becomes difficult, if not impossible, for proper corrective measures to be taken. Unfortunately, we have seen where attempts are made to conceal problems.

- Several Rockwell Hanford officials misled Rockwell and

...AND FOR 25 YEARS OF UNSELFISH SERVICE TO THE SAVANNAH RIVER NUCLEAR WEAPONS PLANT, WE'D LIKE TO PRESENT YOU WITH THIS SMALL TOKEN OF OUR APPRECIATION.

MAINTENANCE

Cartoon by Crowley. Reprinted with permission by Copley News Service.

DOE investigators about the facts surrounding the March 1985 removal of radiation warning signs prior to the visit by Governor Booth Gardner of Washington.

- At the DOE's Feed Materials Production Center near Fernald, Ohio, radon gas was released from waste storage tanks when two steel plates were removed without contractor management approval. The contractor, Westinghouse Materials Company of Ohio, was cited by a DOE incident investigation board as attempting "to prevent disclosure of factual information concerning this incident." DOE Oak Ridge subsequently ordered the removal of the Westinghouse official believed responsible for the attempted coverup.

- DuPont attempted to mislead the DOE as to the reasons why the automatic sprinkler system was turned off at the Tritium Facility. . . .

Desire to Look Good

In an attempt to look good, DOE has hurt its health and safety program by not being completely candid with itself and outsiders. This has resulted in top DOE management not being able to comprehend fully the seriousness of the safety problems that exist. It has also resulted in a loss of credibility. . . .

Root Causes of Safety Problems

DOE's safety problems are due to an imbalance between production and safety. Production demands have forced contractors to cut corners with safety. Other factors include complacency, the inadequacy of the DOE's organizational structure, where the Assistant Secretary for Environment, Safety and Health does not appear to have sufficient independent authority vis-a-vis the operations managers and production people.

Crisis in Leadership

Finally, the staff believes that the DOE is lacking top-level leadership that has both the interest and ability to insure that safety is practiced in a meaningful way. The fact that DOE refused to assist the Subcommittee last August in its review of safety at Savannah River is a case in point. Certain officials were more interested in looking good than in correcting serious safety problems.

WHAT IS POLITICAL BIAS?

This activity may be used as an individualized study guide for students in libraries and resource centers or as a discussion catalyst in small group and classroom discussions.

Many readers are unaware that written material usually expresses an opinion or bias. The skill to read with insight and understanding requires the ability to detect different kinds of bias. Political bias, race bias, sex bias, ethnocentric bias, and religious bias are five basic kinds of opinions expressed in editorials and literature that attempts to persuade. This activity will focus on political bias, defined in the glossary below.

Five Kinds of Editorial Opinion or Bias

SEX BIAS—The expression of dislike for and/or feeling of superiority over the opposite sex or a particular sexual minority.

RACE BIAS—The expression of dislike for and/or feeling of superiority over a racial group.

ETHNOCENTRIC BIAS—The expression of a belief that one's own group, race, religion, culture, or nation is superior. Ethnocentric persons judge others by their own standards and values.

POLITICAL BIAS—The expression of political opinions and attitudes about domestic or foreign affairs.

RELIGIOUS BIAS—The expression of a religious belief or attitude.

Guidelines

Read through the following statements and decide which ones represent political opinions or bias. Evaluate each statement by using the method indicated.

- **Place the letter [P] in front of any sentence that reflects political opinion or bias.**
- **Place the letter [N] in front of any sentence that does not reflect political opinion or bias.**
- **Place the letter [S] in front of any sentence that you are not sure about.**

1. The modernized Nuclear Weapons Complex will be more streamlined and cost effective with the flexibility to adapt to a broad spectrum of potential military, political, and technological futures.

2. Virtually no energy expert thinks our society can remain economically healthy without a growing supply of nuclear power.

3. The Department of Energy has been a strong advocate for safety, and operations at the Department have, when appropriate, been either suspended or modified.

4. In an attempt to look good, the Department of Energy has hurt its health and safety program by not being completely candid with itself and outsiders.

5. The Modernization Plan shows that the entire Nuclear Weapons Complex will require extensive modernization over the next 15-20 years to meet its obligations well into the next century.

6. The safety record of U.S.-style nuclear power plants could not be matched by any other large energy source.

7. The Department of Energy is taking further action to improve safety at the nuclear weapons facilities.

8. Based on its ongoing investigation of safety at the Department of Energy's (DOE) nuclear weapons plants, the Subcommittee staff has found that the safety program at DOE is not working effectively.

9. U.S. nuclear weapons plants must be shut down for good, and the nuclear stockpiles destroyed. All commercial nuclear reactors should be shut down too.

10. We need to halt the spread or proliferation of thermonuclear and biochemical weapons.

11. An environmental disaster, perpetuated by the U.S. government, is taking place at nuclear weapons production plants across the country.

12. American and Soviet policy-makers are rushing to bring additional reactors on line and to introduce supposedly "meltdown-free" models for the 1990s.

Other Activities

1. Locate three examples of political opinion or bias in the readings from Chapter Five.

2. Make up one statement that would be an example of each of the following: *sex bias, race bias, ethnocentric bias, and religious bias.*

3. See if you can locate any factual statements in the twelve items listed above.

BIBLIOGRAPHY I

General Overview of Nuclear Waste

"A Crack Is Reported in S.C. Nuclear Reactor." *Minneapolis Star Tribune,* 18 December 1988, p. 6A.

"Anti-Nuclear Protests May Force Japan to Alter Its Energy Policy." *Minneapolis Star Tribune,* 18 December 1988, p. 18A.

"Arms Plant's Future Hinges on Cleanup, Cash, Governors Say." *Minneapolis Star Tribune*, 17 December 1988.

Boczkiewicz, Robert E. "Prophets and Prayers Rise at Rocky Flats." *National Catholic Reporter*, 2 December 1988, pp. 1-2.

Conner, Chance. "'This Stuff Is Like a Time Bomb.'" *USA Today,* 15 December 1988, p. 1.

Grossman, Dan and Seth Shulman. "The Nuclear-Waste Gamble." *The Progressive,* December 1988, pp. 34-38.

"High Court Sides with States in Nuclear Plant Rate Dispute." *Minneapolis Star Tribune,* 12 January 1989.

Hollyday, Joyce. "In the Valley of the Shadow." *Sojourners*, March 1989, pp. 14-27.

Jaudon, Brian. "In the Shadow of the Bomb." *Sojourners,* 6 January 1989, pp. 5-6.

— — — — — —-. "Pulling the Plug on Nuclear Power." *Sojourners*, March 1989, p. 4.

Johnson, Haynes. "Distant Dangers Don't Make News." *Sojourners*, 12 January 1989.

Kittredge, William. "In My Backyard: A Visit to the Proposed National Nuclear Waste Repository." *Harper's Magazine*, October 1988, pp. 59-63.

Meadows, Donella H. "Nuclear Power Is Not an Atomic Cure For the Greenhouse Effect." *St. Paul Pioneer Press Dispatch,* 4 August 1988, p. 21A.

"New Government Push to Expand Nuclear Power." *The People,* 17 December 1988, p. 3.

"NRDC Demands Impact Statement Before Restart of Weapons Reactors." *NRDC Newsline* (a publication of the Natural Resources Defense Council), Nov/Dec 1988, pp. 1-2.

"Nuclear Power Foes Report Nearly 3,000 Plant Mishaps in '87." *Minneapolis Star Tribune,* 30 December 1988, p. 4A.

"Official: Budget to Have Enough Money to Operate Nuclear Arms Plants Safely." *Minneapolis Star Tribune,* 19 December 1988, p. 10A.

"Radioactive Hazards Used to Push New Bomb Plants." *The People*, 19 November 1988, pp. 1, 8.

Rebuffoni, Dean. "Michigan Halts Plan for Waste Repository." *Minneapolis Star Tribune*, 1 February 1989, p. 5B.

————————. "6 Governors Agree to Do More for Michigan Nuclear Repository." *Minneapolis Star Tribune,* 28 February 1989, p. 8Ae.

Resnikoff, Marvin. *Living Without Landfills*. New York: The Radioactive Waste Campaign, 1988.

Seydel, Robyn. "Opening of N.M. Nuke Dump Is Delayed." *Guardian*, 9 November 1988, p. 4.

"Standing Up for Nuclear Safety." *Minneapolis Star Tribune,* 21 December 1988, p. 20A.

"Start-up of 3 Reactors at Weapons Plant Pushed Back." *Minneapolis Star Tribune*, 28 April 1989.

United States Nuclear Regulatory Commission. "Disposal of Radioactive Waste." Office of Public Affairs, Washington, D.C. 20555.

Wald, Matthew L. "New Radiation Study Planned in Ohio." The *New York Times*, 25 February 1989.

Winebrenner, Denise. "Ohio Battles Nuclear Weapons Plant and DOE." *People's Daily World*, 2 November 1988, p. 4A.

————————. "'We Are Living on a Live Bomb.'" *People's Daily World,* 10 November 1988, p. 19A.

"Yet Another Reactor Incident." *Not Man Apart*, August/September 1988, pp. 1, 6.

BIBLIOGRAPHY II

Radioactive Waste Disposal

These publications may be available at a nearby public or research library.

I. OVERVIEW OF THE PROBLEM

Geological Disposal of Radioactive Waste: An Overview of the Current Status of Understanding and Development. Paris, Organization for Economic Cooperation and Development, 1984, 116 p.

Reports on the status of geological disposal of radioactive wastes. Notes that although high-level radioactive waste requires the long-term isolation of geological disposal, there are alternative methods for low-level waste.

Harrison, J. M. "Disposal of Radioactive Wastes." *Science*, v. 226, 5 October 1984, pp. 11-14.

"Scientists appointed by the International Council of Scientific Unions have concluded that nuclear wastes may be safely disposed of using current technology. Interim storage for 50 to 100 years greatly reduces the problem of thermal loading at the final disposal sites, but more research devoted to such interim storage is needed."

Hileman, Bette. "Nuclear Waste Disposal: A Case of Benign Neglect?" *Environmental Science Technology*, v. 16, May 1982, 271A-275A.

Defines high- and low-level radioactive wastes. Outlines U.S. programs in nuclear waste management.

OECD Nuclear Energy Agency. Radioactive Waste Management Committee. *Technical Appraisal of the Current Situation in the Field of Radioactive Waste Management.* Paris, The Agency, 1985, 47 p.

"The purpose of the present report is: to take stock of the growing scientific understanding and technical progress at national and international levels; and to assess present knowledge in relation to specific policy issues in radioactive waste management and to identify current priority areas."

Zurer, Pamela S. "U.S. Charts Plans for Nuclear Waste Disposal." *Chemical & Engineering News*, v. 61, 18 July 1983, 20-27, 30-38.

Maintains that the technical solutions for safely isolating nuclear waste are available. Calls for the removal of political and institutional roadblocks so this technology can be used effectively.

II. THE U.S. PROGRAM FOR DISPOSAL OF HIGH-LEVEL RADIOACTIVE WASTES

"Best-case Scenario Unlikely; More DOE-NRC Interface Urged." *Nuclear Industry*, v. 32, April 1985, 14-17.

Reviews the status of the nuclear waste repository program. Discusses the Department of Energy's proposal for a monitored retrievable storage (MRS) facility which would be a backup to a permanent repository.

"The Geology of Nuclear Waste Disposal." *Nature,* v. 310, 16 August 1984, pp. 537-540.

"An ICSU [International Council of Scientific Unions] committee on the geological disposal of high-level radioactive wastes has concluded that century-long interim storage is essential and that disposal in subduction trenches and ocean sediments deserves more attention."

Managing Nuclear Waste—A Better Idea. [Washington] U.S. Department of Energy, Advisory Panel on Alternative Means of Financing and Managing Radioactive Waste Facilities, 1984. ca. 244 p. in various pagings.

Reports on the Panel's study of the proposed process for constructing and managing radioactive waste facilities. "The Panel believes that there are several organizational forms, including private corporations, more suited than DOE for managing the construction and operation phases." Makes suggestions for improving the site selection process.

Managing the Nation's Commercial High-level Radioactive Waste. Washington, Office of Technology Assessment, for sale by the Supt. of Docs., G.P.O., 1985. 348 p.

OTA evaluates the Department of Energy's Draft Mission Plan on nuclear waste storage and finds that it falls short of its intended purpose to provide "an informational basis sufficient to permit informed decisions to be made."

Martin, James B. "Managing the Nation's Commercial High-level Radioactive Waste." *Environment,* v. 27, July-August 1985, pp. 25-29.

The reviewer, James B. Martin of the Environmental Defense Fund, asserts that the Nuclear Waste Policy Act process is seriously flawed. He criticizes OTA's report on federal policy for management of high-level waste, for failing to tackle the problems with the DOE waste siting process which lie at the core of the waste disposal program.

Mission Plan for the Civilian Radioactive Waste Management Program: Overview and Current Program Plans. Washington, U.S. Department of Energy, 1984. 1 v. (various pagings) "DOE/RW-OOO5 Draft"

"Volume I and II of II Volumes"

Contents. — Volume I. — Overview and current program plans. — Volume II: Information required by the Nuclear Waste Policy Act of 1982.

Russ, George D., Jr. *Nuclear Waste Disposal: Closing the Circle.* [Bethesda, Md.] Atomic Industrial Forum, 1984. 25 p.

This book "briefly surveys the origin of high-level nuclear waste in power generating reactors as well as its treatment, packaging and transportation for eventual disposal. Emphasis rests, however, on the techniques and technologies employed for setting apart radioactive by-products in deep, mined rock formations."

Salisbury, David F. "Storing Nuclear Waste." *Christian Science Monitor,* 24 June 1985, pp. 1, 6; June 25, pp. 3, 10; June 26, pp. 3, 6; June 27, pp. 3, 6-7; June 28, pp. 3, 8.

Contents.—In search of sites for nuclear waste.—Prospect of nuclear waste dump draws scowls from farmers in Texas panhandle.—Columbia River site, a part of nuclear power's past, may be called on again.—Arid climate and geology bring DOE to one Nevada crest.—As U.S. hunts for atomic waste site, runners-up hold their breath.

U.S. Congressional Budget Office. *Nuclear Waste Disposal: Achieving Adequate Financing;* special study. Washington, C.B.O., 1984. 59 p.

Assesses the Nuclear Waste Policy Act that called for the Department of Energy to develop two geologic repositories for nuclear waste. Examines whether the Nuclear Waste Fund based on a fee now set at 1 mill per kilowatt hour of electricity will be sufficient to cover the cost of development and construction of the waste disposal sites.

U.S. General Accounting Office. *The Nuclear Waste Policy Act: 1984 Implementation Status, Progress, and Problems*; report to the Congress of the United States. Sept. 30, 1985. Washington G.A.O., 1985. 124 p.

"GAO/RCED-85-100"

Examines the Department of Energy's "approach to selecting a waste disposal site, negotiations of agreements with states, and planning for monitored retrievable spent fuel storage."

"West Valley Project Proving that Nuclear Waste Can Be Disposed Safely." *Energy Business,* v. 7, spring 1985, 15-18.

Describes progress at the Department of Energy's demonstration project near Buffalo, N.Y., where liquid high-level nuclear waste is to be converted to borosilicate glass logs which will eventually be stored underground.

III. THE U.S. PROGRAM FOR DISPOSAL OF LOW-LEVEL RADIOACTIVE WASTES

"Disposal of Low-level Radioactive Waste: Impact on the Medical Profession." *JAMA* [Journal of the American Medical Association], v. 254, November 1, 1985, pp. 2449-2451.

"During 1985, low-level radioactive waste disposal has become a critical concern. The issue has been forced by the threatened closure of the three commercial disposal sites." Notes the impact which loss of disposal capacity would have on the medical community's use of radioactive isotopes and urges officials at all levels of government to resolve this issue.

Eng, Raymond, and Jean-Claude F. Dehmel. "Economics of a New Low-level Waste Disposal Facility." *Energy Business,* v. 6, no. 4, 1984, pp. 16-20.

The authors warn states to weigh the economic feasibility of various low-level radioactive waste disposal options. Concludes that large regional disposal sites have significant economies of scale.

Jacobs, Sally. "The Crisis Ahead in Waste Disposal." *New England Business,* v. 6, 17 September 1984, pp. 86-90, 113.

Reviews the status of low-level radioactive waste disposal in the Northeastern states which have been unable to agree on a regional plan required by federal law to be in place by 1986.

Scoville, J. J. "The Obstacles to Low-level Waste Compacts." *Nuclear News*, v. 27, September 1984, pp. 92-100.

Finds many inconsistencies in the 1980 Low-Level Radioactive Waste Disposal Act and in the regional compacts which are being created. Contends that the resulting confusion threatens the national waste disposal system.